The Twelve Steps
And
Dual Disorders

The Twelve Steps
And
Dual Disorders

A framework of recovery
for those of us with addiction
and an emotional or psychiatric illness

Tim Hamilton
Pat Samples

 HAZELDEN®

Hazelden
Center City, Minnesota 55012-0176

Library of Congress Cataloging-in-Publication Data:
Hamilton, Tim.
     The twelve steps and dual disorders : a framework of recovery for
those of us with addiction and an emotional or psychiatric illness /
Tim Hamilton, Pat Samples.
          p.   cm.
     ISBN 1-56838-018-6
     1. Dual diagnosis--Patients--Rehabilitation. 2. Twelve-step
programs. I. Samples, Pat. II. Title.
RC564.68.H35 1994
362.29'186--dc20

                                                        94-8240
                                                           CIP

The Twelve Steps of AA are reprinted and adapted with permission of
Alcoholics Anonymous World Services, Inc. Permission to reprint and adapt
the Twelve Steps does not mean that AA has reviewed or approved the con-
tents of this publication, nor that AA agrees with the views expressed herein.
AA is a program of recovery from alcoholism only—use of the Twelve Steps
in connection with programs and activities that are patterned after AA, but
that address other problems, does not imply otherwise.

Acquisitions Editor: Timothy Quinn McIndoo; Manuscript Editor: Caryn
Pernu; Cover design: David Spohn; Typographer: Deborah Wischow;
Copywriter: Tina Petersen; Production Editor: Cynthia Madsen; Print
Manager: Joan Seim; Printer: Bang Printing; Managing Editor: Donald
Freeman
This book is printed in Caslon

CONTENTS

PREFACE

Tears came to my eyes as I sat in my doctor's office. I was trying to explain to him the great difficulty I was having accepting myself. I felt lost, confused, frightened. For several years, I had been clean and sober. I had even studied and worked in the field of chemical dependency. But clearly something else was very wrong with me. Each year a pattern of disturbing symptoms would recur. At various times, my energy level, mood, attention span, memory, concentration, judgment, sleep, and appetite were all affected. Despite the professional knowledge I had and the tools I was given to assist in my recovery from chemical dependency, I was not prepared to cope with the effects of manic-depressive illness.

The symptoms of my illness were serious, and the problems they caused in my marriage, friendships, school, and work were enormous. But the real damage happened deep within myself. One night my depression led me to decide suicide was more acceptable than continuing my life.

What happened to change my course and lead me to achieve a reasonably well balanced and happy life today?

At first, as my psychiatric illness worsened, I was only aware of the consequences, not of the illness itself. I was filled with ongoing feelings of shame and humiliation, anger and resentment, anxiety and confusion, abandonment and loneliness. I felt more and more hopeless. I was convinced that I was hurting others no matter what I did.

Eventually, my doctor, working with me through much trial and error, was able to treat my psychiatric illness. But it soon became very clear that my two illnesses—manic-depression and addiction—were affecting each other, even though I had received treatment for both. I realized I was a whole person and could not divide my recovery into separate parts for each illness. I wanted to find a way to address the needs of my two disorders in one program, in addition to the separate help I received for each one. I decided to apply the principles of the Twelve Steps to all aspects of my dual disorders. I began to search for others with a similar desire for dual recovery. Together we decided we needed a plan, we needed to meet together and we wanted to create a network to share with others what we were learning. Over time, this group became Dual Recovery Anonymous.

My personal journey of dual recovery has been challenging and rewarding. Some days the psychiatric illness creates greater recovery needs; other days the needs of chemical dependency recovery are greater. But the benefits of dual recovery have been many. Perhaps the greatest benefit has been the way so many others in the program have opened their hearts and shared their courage with me. This book represents my effort to pass along the hope of dual recovery that we share.

—TIM HAMILTON
Director, Dual Recovery Network Association
Contributing author, *The Dual Disorders Recovery Book*

I received a call one day telling me that Dennis, the father of my son's best friend, had killed himself. His son, David, who had been on vacation with his father, was nowhere to be found. After a week-long search that was heart-rending for all of us who knew and loved David (and Dennis), David's body was found. He had been killed by his own dad.

What drove this man to destroy his own life and his son's? No one can answer that for certain. What is known is that Dennis suffered from a psychiatric illness and from chemical dependency. Although he was no longer drinking and attended Alcoholic Anonymous meetings regularly, he was not taking his prescribed medications and had been unstable and prone to both depression and violent behavior. Treatment for one of his

serious illnesses did not take care of the other. He had probably never heard of treating these two life-threatening illnesses
in combination through dual recovery. If he had, perhaps the
tragic deaths of two wonderful people might have been
avoided.

I agreed to assist Tim Hamilton in writing this book because
I believe so deeply in the power of the Twelve Steps. Even
though I do not personally experience the dual disorders of
chemical dependency and an emotional or psychiatric illness, I
welcomed the opportunity to contribute my writing talents to
offer hope to those who do. No one should have to reach the
level of despair and desperation that I believe Dennis did. *The
Twelve Steps and Dual Disorders* offer a way out. Much to my
surprise, while working on this book, I discovered how the
same Steps could help me personally with my own dual disorders of compulsive eating and an anxiety disorder.

—PAT SAMPLES
Co-author, *Self-Care for Caregivers: A Twelve Step Approach*
and author of other recovery literature

DUAL RECOVERY:
BASICS TO BUILD ON

The purpose of this book is to offer those of us who are affected by dual disorders a way to recover. Our disorders are called "dual" because we are affected in two ways: (1) we are chemically dependent, and (2) we experience an emotional or psychiatric illness.

Not only are we affected by these separate and independent illnesses, we find there is yet another problem. The two illnesses interact with one another. As a result:

- The two illnesses may become more difficult to diagnose.
- The illnesses may worsen, and treatment may become more difficult.
- Recovery may become more difficult to maintain, leading to (1) a relapse to using alcohol or other addictive drugs, or (2) a return or worsening of psychiatric symptoms.

Having dual disorders presents us with a tremendous set of risks if we do not take seriously our need to recover. But recovery from dual disorders can get sidetracked by a complicated series of roadblocks unless we take a realistic approach to recovery.

Dual recovery, a realistic approach to coping with the problems of a dual disorder, is based on two simple ideas:

- We treat *both* our chemical dependency and our emotional or psychiatric illness.
- We follow a personal recovery program that helps us combine and balance the needs of both.

Those of us in dual recovery each have a unique story and set of circumstances. We are all affected differently.

- Some of us have had difficulty perceiving reality clearly. We may have experienced hallucinations, either hearing voices or seeing visions.
- Others have felt greatly increased energy. We have experienced changes in our ability to think and make judgments. Our thoughts sometimes race and seem to go out of control.
- Some of us have experienced a loss of energy, a loss of enjoyment of life, and a persistently gloomy outlook. Perhaps our sleeping patterns and appetite have changed. We may have become suicidal. We may have had difficulties with thoughts and concentration.
- Still others have experienced repeated rushes of uncontrollable anxiety that include a rapid heart beat, shortness of breath, and feeling faint.

This list is far from complete. Our symptoms vary greatly, but they point to a common bond: we experience no-fault illnesses that seriously disrupt our ability to function and relate to others effectively.

Some of us are extremely disabled by our psychiatric illness, and we live in group homes or other supportive environments. Others, despite trying very hard to manage the psychiatric illness, have suffered from a repeated return of symptoms because of problems with medications or other difficulties. Still others have achieved considerable relief and stability through counseling, self-help support, and the appropriate use of psychiatric medications or other forms of treatment.

We also found we had some differences in our abuse of alcohol or other drugs. Some of us drank only in certain places or with certain people or at certain times. The frequency and amount we used varied widely. Some of us hid our use of drugs from others. Some of us drove while intoxicated or broke other laws. Some of us drank or used drugs only at home. We may have been through treatment once, or many times, or not at all.

Despite our differences, however, we have found that we have much in common. Each illness has symptoms that interfere with our ability to function effectively and relate to ourselves and others. Our impaired functioning has created a series of problems and consequences for us, and we have responded by trying to protect ourselves in unhealthy ways. The way we coped with feelings and problems very often became self-defeating or self-destructive. We learned to adapt to our illnesses and live with them rather than seek help—until we found dual recovery.

The goals for dual recovery are probably similar for each of us whether we are seeking help for the first time or coming back to try again. We want to

- stop the pain and confusion caused by the symptoms of our illnesses, the consequences and problems our symptoms create, and our ineffective means of coping
- maintain a safe recovery and prevent relapse
- improve the quality of our lives

Those goals are the focus of the Twelve Steps, a program for dual recovery. Some of us come to dual recovery already familiar with the Twelve Step approach to recovery. Others have no experience with the Twelve Steps or perhaps have some misconceptions about this approach. Before moving on, it may be helpful to review some basics.

The Twelve Steps for Dual Recovery is a plan that we can follow to help us organize and structure our resources and the direction of our recovery. The plan is divided into Twelve Steps, which are suggestions rather than rules. The Steps are based on our freedom to develop personal beliefs and lifestyles for recovery. They offer us new opportunities for healthy change and learning and new ways to view ourselves and our illnesses. They guide us in rebuilding our lives and relationships and lead us from being victims of our dual illnesses to claiming the responsibility for our own recovery. The stories and support of others in the program guide us and give us a reason to hope.

Actions are suggested for working each Step. These include reading program literature; reviewing our own beliefs, behaviors, and emotions; writing down what we discover; and talking with people we trust and people who care about us. The Twelve Steps offer a variety of tools to help us review options and make choices to improve our lives. As we become more grounded in our own recovery, we can begin helping other people recover as well.

The Twelve Steps for Dual Recovery also offer suggestions for maintaining recovery and preventing relapse. They teach us about the effectiveness of using reminders, recognizing warning signs, and taking appropriate action. We can use these tools in all areas of our lives.

Over time, if we are faithful to dual recovery, we find ourselves growing and changing. Our understanding, beliefs, and philosophies change. Our need for structure or for flexibility changes. We become happier people. We find greater peace of mind.

This book offers you an invitation to walk along this path of dual recovery that has helped so many of us. Having both chemical dependency and a psychiatric illness can be too much to bear alone. Trying to treat each separately does not work. Treating them together, in the company of others who are recovering, opens the way for greater peace of mind.

Some readers of this book may be experiencing an addictive disorder other than chemical dependency, such as compulsive gambling, spending, or eating, along with an emotional or psychiatric illness. If this is your case, you may find the principles of dual recovery discussed in this book just as helpful for you.

STEP ONE

*We admitted we were powerless over our dual illness of chemical dependency and emotional or psychiatric illness—that our lives had become unmanageable.**

Step One is a groundwork Step. We begin to recognize and accept our present condition. We admit that we experience both chemical dependency and a psychiatric illness and that our lives have been greatly affected because of this dual disorder. We see clearly that without help we cannot recover from these illnesses. Alone, we will not be able to prevent relapse—a return to the use of alcohol or other drugs or a return of our psychiatric symptoms—because of the lack of proper self-care.

Step One is a new beginning. Once we lay the groundwork of acceptance, we can begin the gentle process of recovery from each illness. Our recovery becomes an "inside job." We recognize within ourselves what we *can* change our beliefs, emotions, and behaviors, and we take responsibility for that. We give up trying to change what we can't, especially the aspects of our illnesses that are beyond our control.

Why Step One is needed
We are addicted

Somewhere in the course of our lives, something happened that changed us forever. The desire for the highly pleasurable effects of alcohol or other drugs began to be more and more important in our lives. For some of us, the urge became extreme. The thought of using was with us most of the time. We couldn't wait until the next opportunity to drink or use drugs. The urge to have the desired effects was overpowering.

Or the experience may have been more subtle. We may have

*The Twelve Steps of Dual Recovery Anonymous are adapted from the Twelve Steps of Alcoholics Anonymous. The complete Twelve Steps of Alcoholics Anonymous and Dual Recovery Anonymous appear on pages 98 and 99.

told ourselves, I just feel like drinking or getting high. More and more, we found ourselves choosing to be around friends who used. We frequented places where alcohol and drugs were available. Pretty soon we were regularly using more than we wanted to.

Whether our preoccupation and desire to get high were blatant or subtle, our excessive use of alcohol or other drugs gradually created problems for us and others around us. Yet when we finally recognized that something was going wrong with us, we couldn't stop ourselves from taking that next drink or hit. We had crossed a line. We were addicted to alcohol or other intoxicating drugs. Our addiction did not develop because we had been drinking or using too much, but because something in our body chemistry created a compelling craving that most other people do not experience. Despite our growing inability to stop drinking or using, however, when anyone suggested we had a problem with these drugs, we denied it. We could not see what was happening to us. This is also part of addiction—denial.

We have an emotional illness

Something else also changed our lives forever. Another illness began to develop. Whether suddenly or gradually, we began to notice we were not experiencing life in our normal way. Perhaps this change began with minor symptoms, such as headaches, anxiety, difficulty sleeping or eating, or problems with memory or concentration. The problems didn't seem all that big at first and the possibility of psychiatric illness didn't occur to us. We tried to ignore the symptoms, or perhaps we tried to get help from a doctor or therapist. But because some of our symptoms would keep changing or come and go, or because we were drinking or using drugs, we had trouble getting an accurate diagnosis and proper treatment. If we did get the right kind of help, perhaps we didn't always follow through by taking medications or participating in other treatment consistently. We thought we could manage without help.

Gradually our symptoms and our ability to cope with them got more and more out of hand. We each reacted differently, depending on the nature of our particular illness. Some of us felt too overwhelmed to function. Because of our impaired judgment, some of us had episodes in which we became involved in plans and projects that left us financially bankrupt. Some of us had increasing hallucinations (hearing voice or seeing visions) or delusions (greatly distorted views of reality) that disrupted our lives. Many of us got to the point where we felt exhausted and broken. We had trouble sleeping and our appetite was poor. We felt irritable, our memory and concentration were poor, and our quality of life was deteriorating. Some of us attempted suicide. All of us became unable to manage our lives the way we wanted to, and we felt powerless over our condition.

We have two no-fault disorders

We have two serious illnesses to recover from. Both are no-fault illnesses. We didn't do anything to cause them. Neither one caused the other. We can't make either one go away. They are two different illnesses, each with its own symptoms, each creating its own set of problems, each needing special types of treatment. Yet we cannot separate our illnesses into tidy little compartments within ourselves. Both are present within us. Each influences the other. Both cause us to "lose control." The loss of control caused by these two diseases together becomes overpowering. If we drink or use other drugs, we may become careless about our recovery and neglect to take our medications or to participate in other needed treatment. As a result, the symptoms of our mental illness return or worsen. On the other hand, if we don't tend to our mental illness properly, the symptoms will worsen. We may then withdraw and fail to seek the support we need to keep from relapsing to the use of alcohol or other drugs or other addictive behaviors.

We are out of control in our use of alcohol and other drugs

In Step One, we come face to face with our dual illness. We admit we have not managed to control our two conditions successfully, despite countless efforts. To control our chemical dependency, we have tried to drink or use only at certain times or in certain places. But we have been unable to keep those limits, despite our best intentions. We have felt genuine regret over the harm that we have caused those we love. We have condemned ourselves, hoping that feelings of guilt and remorse would cause us to stop or cut back. But we only lost control again, and felt more guilty and ashamed. We hid our liquor or other drugs, persuaded ourselves that "just one" wouldn't hurt, got angry when others confronted us, made promises of reform, and offered excuses. Again and again, we lost control.

We are out of control in our psychiatric illness

We tried many ways to control our psychiatric or emotional illness too. We tried to toughen up our mental attitude, believing that "mind over matter" would solve the problem. But we quickly found our illness could not be controlled by willpower. We may have tried one or two medications but then gave up when they didn't quickly control our symptoms or had unpleasant side effects. Rather than improving our treatment program, we got angry at doctors and decided we could manage on our own. But the symptoms worsened. At times, we assumed that friends and family members would take care of us. At other times, we refused their help and resented their intrusion. In either case, we found no relief from our symptoms, and we often alienated those who loved us. Sometimes we tried to just forget about our mental and emotional illness, but the symptoms and related problems haunted us no matter how hard we tried. Some of us even took an overdose of medication, hoping to end the pain once and for all. But it did not.

We tried separate treatment

Sometimes we became very responsible about one of our illnesses. We sought professional help, followed the recommended treatment program, and achieved partial recovery. But we ignored the other illness. For example, we assumed that if we were sober, our mental and emotional problems might clear up. They didn't. In fact, sometimes they got worse or became more obvious.

At times we sought treatment for our psychiatric illness, thinking that if we were mentally and emotionally stable, our craving for alcohol or other drugs would go away. It did not. We have an addiction for chemicals that is separate from our mental illness. Even when we pursued treatment for both illnesses, few of us learned how to deal with the combined effects of the two illnesses.

In all cases, we found that we were powerless over our dual illnesses by ourselves. We couldn't stop drinking or using. We couldn't find mental or emotional stability. We were desperate, out of answers.

Our lives became unmanageable

One way we discovered our powerlessness was by noticing how unmanageable our lives had become—sometimes to an extreme degree. Our abilities seemed to be slipping away. We could not concentrate, could not remember, could not make sound decisions. Emotionally, we felt burned out, disconnected, unhappy. Physically, we may have injured ourselves, we were often tired, and we suffered from a variety of ailments resulting from our illnesses.

In our relationships, we felt like failures. Perhaps our children could not count on us or suffered in other ways from our extreme emotional reactions. Spouses, partners, or roommates ran out of patience as we became withdrawn for long periods or used up the household resources or insisted on pursuing highly irrational activities. Parents and other caregivers no longer would help us through one more crisis or pick us up from emergency rooms, detox centers, or jails. We lost friends. We felt misunderstood and rejected and we gave up on them all. Yet we knew we had been unfair to them. We felt ashamed.

Life was also unmanageable at school and on the job. We may have missed deadlines and been sullen and uncooperative. We showed great enthusiasm one day and apathy the next. We tried to hide from others what we were going through. Yet we showed up drunk or high, hungover, late, or not at all. If we heard voices, music, or other sounds, we may have talked about our hallucinations, expecting others to believe us or understand. If anyone suggested that our behavior was a problem, our temper flared and we looked for a scapegoat.

Sometimes we would tell people, "I'm going to get myself together now." We tried sincerely, but again and again we found we were powerless. The two illnesses didn't go away. The symptoms recurred and interfered with our lives. We could not manage to live the lives we wanted to.

We protected our feelings with denial

With two such challenging illnesses, we quickly found ways to protect our feelings. We slipped into denial. Having either a psychiatric illness or chemical dependency was hard enough for us to accept. But the thought of having two illnesses seemed entirely too much to bear.

One problem was that both illnesses had some degree of social stigma attached to them. Some people hinted—or told us directly—that we were morally weak, that we had done something to cause our illnesses, or that we were just manipulating others. None of this is true; yet such stigma and prejudice can hurt deeply. We did not want to deal with such feelings, and we did not want to deal with any of the consequences of our illnesses. Therefore, it seemed easier simply to deny we had one or both of these illnesses, or to deny their seriousness. But over and over again, the symptoms and their consequences continued to recur.

How Step One works

We admit we are powerless

When we face the truth about our dual illnesses, recovery begins. We become honest. The pain and the desire for a better life both become so great that we quit trying to hide. We no longer pretend we are in control of the situation. We stop asking others to put up with our damaging behavior. We begin to take responsibility for recovery from our dual disorders. We know we deserve a better life. We start to trust that dual recovery is possible for us, even though we do not know how as yet.

The Twelve Step program starts simply. We admit that we are powerless over having these two illnesses and powerless over how they affect each other. We acknowledge our symptoms, and we acknowledge that our lives have become chaotic and unmanageable.

Then we stop blaming anyone for what is happening. If we had high blood pressure and heart disease, chances are we would neither ignore them nor blame anyone for them. We would not try to treat either one without understanding its relation to the other. By the same token, we neither ignore our chemical dependency and psychiatric illness nor blame anyone for them. We acknowledge we have these dual disorders, we learn what we can about them, and we take measures to treat them. Only by accepting the truth and taking responsible action do we find freedom. Only then can we can live a balanced, useful life and be at peace with ourselves.

We recognize our goodness and choose recovery
Step One starts us on the responsible, gentle process of recovery. We recognize that we are not bad people, but good people with two very serious but treatable illnesses. We come to realize that we have been through a trauma, and we give ourselves credit for all we have done up to this point to better our lives. It has not been easy for us; not everybody gets this far. Yet we no longer feel sorry for ourselves. Instead, we decide to use healthy ways to treat our dual illnesses from now on. We become willing to do whatever it takes to recover. We are patient with ourselves in the process because we know change takes time. Yet we take the Twelve Steps to heart and work them every day, one day at a time.

The tools to help us
We have found one or more tools that help us work each of the Twelve Steps. Some are specific, practical measures that make the ideas in this program concrete. Some are overall attitudes or other resources that help us keep a positive perspective as we work the step. By using these tools, we increase our chances of dual recovery.

Meetings with others
At first, the thought of admitting powerlessness can be very frightening: What does this mean? What will I have to do?

Fortunately, we do not have to face these questions alone. We can find many others who share similar experiences and feelings and who are willing to recover. If it is possible, we begin meeting with others who want to work on dual recovery in a program based on the Twelve Steps. If we can find only one person to share our journey of recovery with, we do that. It only takes two people to start a meeting. In sharing with others, we find our strength.

Our history

To begin our recovery, we need to have a good understanding of our dual disorders. In Step One, we want to get a clear picture of each illness. We recall when each illness started and we follow its progression to the present. We particularly note how the two illnesses affected each other.

In examining the history of our dual disorders, we recall the symptoms we experienced. We recall how they interfered with our ability to function and relate to others. We note the problems and consequences that resulted. How did they affect our work performance? How did they change our relationships? What were the physical consequences over time? We recall our hospitalizations. We recall our various counseling experiences and treatments, including medications. We remember our different attempts to get control of our dual illnesses. We note the ways we tried to protect ourselves from being hurt emotionally. What did we do to hide our illnesses from other people? How was our self-image affected? We look at how we gradually adapted to the illness rather than treat it responsibly. We acknowledge the great difficulty and chaos our illnesses have created. We look into all areas of our lives and note where we have become disabled. We look to see when the symptoms of our illnesses recurred. We pay attention to the patterns in each illness.

With this personal history, we gain a much clearer picture of our lives as they really are today. We don't try to analyze our dual disorders or search for causes, we simply establish that the illnesses and the associated problems are real. That way we know where we are starting from. We have a clear sense of how seriously our condition has damaged our lives. We start to see the areas that we can change and those we can't.

Three simple ideas

Three simple ideas guide us in dual recovery. They are expressed in daily affirmations that remind ourselves that our goal is peace of mind:

- Today I will be free of alcohol and other intoxicating drugs.
- Today I will follow a healthy plan to manage my emotional or psychiatric illness.
- Today I will practice the Twelve Steps to the best of my ability.

Barriers to overcome

Shock

We may feel a great deal of resistance when we first become aware of our dual disorder and our powerlessness over this condition. We may think, It can't be true!. It seems so unfair! I don't deserve this. I'm too young. This is too much to handle.

Such reactions are common. Finding out that we have any major illness, let alone two major illnesses, is a shock. Suddenly we feel we have lost something we had long hoped for—to be "normal" someday, like everybody else. We are face to face with the reality that our lives may have changed for good.

The stages of adjustment

Our reaction to this change follows the course that is common to any adjustment to unexpected change—first denial, then anger, bargaining, sadness and mourning, and finally acceptance. We have already discussed denial, the belief that it's simply not true that we have two disorders. We are convinced, and we try to convince others, that we are not sick, or at least not that sick. We look for a way to make the problem go away. We're convinced there must be some other explanation. But the problem persists.

Then we become outraged that this could happen to us. We

are angry at God, our parents, the doctors, and others we think are to blame, even ourselves. Our fury may be long and loud, or we may hold it inside ourselves, but we resent what has happened.

Next we try bargaining, maneuvering, and manipulating our way out. Maybe if we just get a little more rest, try a little harder to concentrate, drink a little less, change jobs, break off a relationship, or switch drugs, everything will settle down and get back to normal. Perhaps we decide to go on "one last drunk," thinking that then we will be ready to give it up for good.

When reality sets in and we see once again that both illnesses are here to stay, we experience feelings of sadness and mourn our losses. Perhaps we can no longer perform on the job the way we once could. Perhaps we fear that our creativity will wane if we use medications to control our manic episodes. Perhaps the medications we need affect our sexual functioning or our weight. We may look back and see that our illnesses have taken so much of our time and attention that we have lost important relationships, opportunities for personal development, or the chance to enjoy our children as they grew up.

With patience, and with our willingness to work Step One, we reach a point of acceptance. We accept both the dual disorders and the problems they have caused us and others. We choose to recover by learning how to live with them in serenity one day at a time.

Benefits

A way out

Step One gets us unstuck. It gives us the ability to move forward. We can see the patterns in our history that have trapped us over and over again. And we can begin to see the way out of these destructive patterns.

The freedom to recover

Step One moves us into freedom. We can live a life in dual recovery. Instead of fighting our condition constantly, we accept that it does exist and we learn to manage our recovery. We see what we need to do, and we do it. Of course, working Step One does not mean we never again have problems. We will still have some of the symptoms of our illnesses. We will still have the urge to use at times. But we have begun the journey of recovery. We are learning how to cope with these challenges and find some peace of mind.

Stepping forward

Once we take Step One, we become clearer about what has really been happening to us and what we are coping with. Next we look ahead to see where we are going and what tools will help us get there. We start to examine what sanity means and how to achieve it. We begin to identify a source of help for our dual recovery that we can believe in.

STEP TWO

Came to believe that a Higher Power of our understanding could restore us to sanity.

In Step Two, we identify a source of help and direction for sane living. This Step is an opportunity to loosen the grip our dual disorders have held on our lives. Because of our illnesses, we have felt unsound or insane. Now we can let go of our unsound and insane ways and take hold of our lives again.

To restore our sanity, we become willing to believe in a source of help we can call our Higher Power or Helping Power. It is a Higher Power that we identify for ourselves and choose freely, one that seems workable and makes sense to us. We choose a source of help that we honestly believe we can work with to bring order to our lives and give us peace of mind.

Why Step Two is needed

We suffer from a chemical imbalance

In Step One, we examined the progression of our dual disorders, and we saw how unmanageable and insane our lives had become. That insanity takes two forms—insanity that stems from our body chemistry and insanity that is based on unsound judgment, or "stinking thinking."

Many psychiatric illnesses are believed to result from a chemical imbalance in the body. This imbalance may produce a wide range of symptoms, impairments, and disabilities. If we are hallucinating (whether seeing things or hearing voices), depressed, anxious, compulsive, or manic, our soundness and sanity are certainly called in question. We may easily make poor judgments. Our coping becomes impaired. We become immobilized or live in constant chaos or simply get by from one day to the next.

We fall into stinking thinking

Another form of our insanity is the way we cope with our illness. Our beliefs, behaviors, and emotions can influence us in ways that are self-defeating. Whether we call it unsound judgment, insanity, or stinking thinking, we have habits of thought, coping patterns, and attitudes that keep our lives out of balance, our minds out of touch with reality. Stinking thinking puts us at risk for returning to alcohol or other drugs and for reexperiencing our psychiatric symptoms. The clearest example of unsound judgment is that we continue to use alcohol and other intoxicating drugs, believing we can be in control, despite our many failed attempts in the past and despite the devastating effects. Another example is that we discontinue the appropriate use of our psychiatric medications, even though each time we have done so in the past our symptoms return.

Unsound judgment or stinking thinking, then, is any attitude or action that puts us at risk for relapsing to chemical use or for neglecting the treatment plan for our emotional illness. For example, we may keep hanging around with friends who drink or use, or we may withdraw from people who can help us—or both. We look for these patterns of thinking and behaving more clearly in Steps Four and Ten, our inventory Steps.

With dual disorders, we can easily get caught up in the negative opinions and prejudices others have about us and come to believe the social stigma is justified. We go along when others blame or shame us for being sick. If people call us nuts, schizo, lazy, a freeloader, psycho, a bum, or a self-pitying whiner, we accept their definition of us. Or we stay in the closet about our illness and recovery. When we hear people using prejudicial language, we remain quiet and feel the pain.

When both illnesses are active, the insanity of the two often overlaps. We may use depression or anxiety or paranoia as an excuse for our relapse to alcohol or other drugs, despite knowing that using will only make matters worse. Or using chemicals may cause us to neglect treating our psychiatric illness appropriately, resulting in a recurrence of our psychiatric symptoms.

In Step Two, we come to believe that we can get out of this double insanity—with help. That's where our source of help, our Higher Power, comes in: to offer us direction, to help us rebuild a saner life.

How Step Two works

We create a picture of sanity

What, then, is sanity, and how do we get there? We each have to answer this question for ourselves. If we were living a sane life, how would our life be different than it is now? What would we be like? We would no longer have to hang on to distorted, hopeless, chaotic, fearful, grandiose, and reckless views of life. Having a realistic picture of sanity for ourselves is important. If we don't know what sanity is, how can we ever expect to achieve it?

Some of us recovering from dual disorders picture sanity as simply liking ourselves, feeling healthy, and having plenty of natural energy. We imagine ourselves talking clearly, finishing sentences. Our thoughts are clear. We are not unreasonably fearful. We are able to handle intrusive and harmful thoughts. We readily stay away from alcohol and other intoxicating drugs. We take care of ourselves, and we are able to complete the tasks we are responsible for. We cope reasonably well with our illnesses and with other problems that come up. Our vision of sanity includes having relationships that are open, honest, and respectful. We see ourselves as creative and able to follow up on things without being especially impulsive or compulsive.

You may adopt these ideas about sanity or find other ways to define it. If you are new to the program, you may not be at all sure yet what sanity is. You may also be fearful that you will never be any more sane than you are now. In time, by working Step Two, you can be confident that your vision of sanity will become clearer. What is important for now is that you begin with some idea of how your life could be saner. You may ask, Is it too early for me to be picturing my life in the future? Yet you have already started that process by seeking help through this program. Most of us have also tried other means, such as hospitalization or treatment, to reduce our pain and improve the quality of our life. Having seen the success of others in dual recovery, we can be assured that we are moving in the right direction, a sane direction.

We set new directions

Once we have a picture of sanity, we begin to move in new directions. We decide what changes we will make so our lives will more closely match the new picture. Step Two mainly involves coming to a new belief in a better life; the new directions we choose are a way to make that belief concrete. Perhaps we decide to establish a new daily routine that includes rising on schedule, exercising, eating well, dressing in a way that makes us feel good about ourselves, and following any prescribed treatment regimen.

We ask ourselves, What kind of helpful attitude can I adopt about my living situation? About my work? About my illnesses?

Would it be helpful to make changes in my relationships? What qualities can I look for in the people I choose to associate with? Are there some people I need to say no to? Are there some people I need to treat with more respect?

What plans can I make for my future? Education? A different job? More structure? More flexibility?

Ask yourself what it will take to move in these new directions. The more specific your plans, the better. Write them down. Discuss them with people you trust, people who care about you.

Take your time in deciding on the changes you need to make. You may start with just one or two ideas.

We identify a Higher Power

In Step Two, we come to believe in a Higher Power of our understanding. This Step stresses freedom and independent choice. We make our recovery program personal by choosing our own source of help and deciding how we will work with it. We turn inward and ask ourselves what power we are willing to trust as a source of help to restore our sanity.

There are many ways to define a Higher or Helping Power.

Some of us turn to the traditions of our childhood and choose a Higher Power such as God, Allah, or Great Spirit. Others find a Higher Power in a new religious faith. Some choose the Creator of the world or Nature itself as a Higher Power, because such a concept represents universal order and harmony. And some of us choose a more personal Higher Power, a spirit we believe is present within us and cares for us and guides our way.

Those of us with severe and persistent forms of psychiatric illness may not feel comfortable seeking a religious or spiritual Higher Power. During our illness, we may have seen angels, demons, or human religious figures, such as Jesus. Or we may have had the thought that we were, in fact, God. If we have experienced these kinds of delusions, we may need special help to identify a Higher Power. We can turn to someone more experienced in the program, perhaps a sponsor, to help us sort out our delusions from reality and to help us develp a concept of a Higher Power that fits our needs.

Another way to think about a Higher Power is as time. Time is a great helper and healer. We know that in time we can learn all we need to learn, we can practice the Steps, and we can heal.

We are not limited to identifying a single source of help. We can think about a Higher Power as a personal committee or a circle of support. This committee or circle might consist of the resources we have that promote our recovery. These resources may include a spiritual source such as God, our caseworker or counselor, our medication, healing techniques, the Twelve Steps, our sponsor, Twelve Step meetings and literature, and any other source of help we value. We are in the center of the circle. We make the choice to draw on the resources that make up our Higher Power committee or circle.

You can choose among these definitions of a Higher Power or come up with your own. What is important is to choose a Higher Power that you trust as a personal source of help for you—a concept that makes at least some sense to you and that provides caring, positive support. Don't worry about making a wrong choice. Just begin, and trust that in time your picture of the right Higher Power for you will become clearer. Remember, we can change our choice at any time. As we learn and grow in the program, we may also change how we work with our Higher Power.

The tools to help us
Good, organized direction

Working Step Two, we automatically begin to get our life in better order. We choose our new directions, we call on all the available resources, and we begin to believe in ourselves again. As we face each life situation, we ask ourselves, Is this good for me and my dual recovery? Does it make sense? Do the pieces all fit together? Does it move me in a direction that is consistent with my recovery?

The slogans

Two slogans common to Twelve Step programs are especially helpful in working Step Two.

First things first. We take this Step in an orderly way, one thing at a time. We do the necessary work of exploring our insanity and deciding if we are ready to give it up. We consider what sanity is and choose new directions. We examine our view of God and religion from our past and see whether that view best fits our need for a Higher Power now. We listen to the experience of others in the program. Then we make a deliberate choice about an appropriate Power to help us. We place our faith in that Power. By working the Step in an orderly manner like this, we already begin to establish a sense of greater order in our lives.

Easy does it. This is a gentle program. We try not to put pressure on ourselves. We do the best we can. We believe when we are ready. If believing seems difficult, we "act as if" we believe, to help get us started. We want what the program offers, and we move toward it at our own pace.

Barriers to overcome
Past religious difficulties

If we had a bad experience with religion in the past, we may hesitate to embrace anything that reminds us of religion or

God. We can set aside that hesitation when we realize that we are free to define our Higher Power for ourselves—one that is totally caring and supportive of us.

Reluctance to trust again

We have tried so many things to help us feel better—religion, counseling, self-discipline, treatment, medical answers—and we still relapsed or came close to it. Yes, trusting again is a risk. But others in dual recovery can remind us that we have all had that hesitation, and that those of us who went ahead and took Step Two anyway are now living saner lives.

Benefits

New hope

Step Two moves us from feeling helpless to feeling hopeful. It is the beginning of renewed self-worth. We no longer have to feel like a number in the medical system, or in any other system. We take hold of our lives and choose sanity over insanity. We now have a Higher Power that we have chosen and that we believe in to help us carry out the plan for recovery offered by the Twelve Steps. We are on our way.

Gradual, gentle healing

Things don't all change right away, but over time something special happens when we keep believing in our Higher Power and working the rest of the Twelve Steps. We can't expect magic, but through trial and error, we discover how well this program works. We find it to be comprehensive. It addresses both of our illnesses and guides us through a gentle healing process in all areas of our lives—personal growth, daily living issues, relationships with family and others, physical health, spirituality, and work concerns. As a result, we live more directed, balanced lives.

Sanity

Identifying and believing in a Higher Power helps us restore our sanity. By *sanity* we mean

- *Physical sanity,* so we can manage the symptoms of a chemical imbalance or another type of illness.
- *Sanity in our beliefs and behavior,* so we can get beyond self-defeating and self-destructive ways of relating to ourselves and others.
- *Sanity of spirit,* so we are motivated to choose life rather than suicide or resignation to chance and circumstance. We find an inner strength and motivation that fuels our longing for recovery rather than losing ourselves more and more in the grip of our symptoms.

Stepping forward

With Step Two, we find new hope through belief in a Higher Power of our own choosing. Now we are ready to make the all-important choice—to leave behind our insanity and begin acting in concert with the Power we have found.

STEP THREE

Made a decision to turn our will and our lives over to the care of our Higher Power, to help us to rebuild our lives in a positive and caring way.

Step Three is a turning point. We've identified the problem (powerlessness, insanity). We've identified a source of help. Now it's time to take action.

In Step Three, we make a simple but all-important commitment. We decide to let go of our old, ineffective ways and begin to look to our new source of help—our Higher Power—for the guidance and resources we need for dual recovery. We decide to move into a new, saner way of living.

Step Three does not directly treat or cure our chemical dependency or psychiatric illness. Rather, it helps us manage our dual disorders. It gives us hope that dual recovery is possible. We find new courage and strength. We begin to restore our lives. We move toward the vision of recovery that we formed in Step Two.

Why Step Three is needed

Our success has been limited

For a long time, we have been trying to find peace of mind by ourselves. We have made endless plans and promises: I'm going to get it together. I'll never get myself in that situation again.

But our ways of coping have been self-defeating. We slip into stinking thinking, making excuses for why things did not work out and avoiding help: I'll change drugs, break off my relationship, and drink only after 6:00 P.M. It's only stress (or my job or my family); when that changes, things will get better.

On our own, our success has been very limited. Many times we have ended up feeling worse.

Step Three frees us from our limitations. We don't have to work so hard at getting better any more. We can let go and let our Higher Power smooth the way for us.

The going has been rough

Making the choice to work Step Three is like planning the perfect vacation. Do we want to drive along rock-filled, avalanche-prone roads in a battered 1960 Volkswagen with bald tires? Or would we rather drive a new Jaguar along a smooth highway? We have a choice. Either way we still have to decide on our destination and make the effort to drive the car. But with the Jaguar, we are much more certain of arriving at our destination in good health and in good time.

How Step Three works

We use our new Power

What does it mean to turn our will and our lives over to our Higher Power? It's like stepping into the Jaguar. We go ahead and use the best means we can to get where we want to go. We follow directions that come from our Higher Power, whether our chosen Higher Power is spiritual, physical, medical, or some combination of these. In Step Two, we chose a good, orderly direction for our lives, based on the program, the Steps, and the personal goals we set. Now we start to apply ourselves toward achieving our goals. We have a new Power to help us do this, and we call on this source of help in everything we do.

Of course, this means we have to change the way we've always done things. We have to let go of the familiar, even though it hasn't worked very well. We have to take hold of what works, even though we have doubts. If we have felt sorry for ourselves because of our illness, we become willing to accept what has happened and we keep our focus on making the best of the present. If we used drugs as a way of building up our courage or dulling our pain, we learn from our Higher Power how to find authentic courage and reduce our pain in safe ways. If others have given up on us, we rely on the one who believes in us—our Higher Power—and on the plans we have made to help us believe in ourselves.

We develop a relationship

We develop a working relationship with our Higher Power. We put our trust there. We rely on our Higher Power to direct and support us, and we are not disappointed.

For our part, we do our best to be honest and open. We become willing to accept the direction given to us. We ask for guidance, we wait, we listen, and we take action, practicing our new way of doing things. Like any relationship, this one takes time to develop, and we get out of the relationship what we put into it. We learn to work with our Higher Power much as we would work with an unbeatable coach, making every effort to carry out a winning game plan for ourselves. We turn our will and our lives over throughout the day. Gradually, our lives are reshaped in a way that builds strong recovery.

We listen for the guidance

If making a connection with our Higher Power is new to us, we may need time to get used to this idea. We may not be sure how to recognize the guidance. How does it come to us? How can we tell if what we hear is just our old, sick thinking or truly guidance from our Higher Power?

The guidance we receive is often obvious and practical. Our Higher Power may work through the people, events, and other resources in our lives. We may get help through a new medical advance, the example of a friend, the wisdom in a book, the advice of a doctor, or the opportunity for just the right job. Whatever comes our way, we check within ourselves in quiet reflection to see if what is coming is best for us. Does it promote our highest good? As we become more experienced in checking within ourselves, we learn to trust our inner sense of what is right for us. We learn to use the guidance we receive.

For some people, guidance comes mainly during times of prayer or quiet reflection. We may feel a gentle nudging inside to make some constructive, healthy choice for ourselves. Regardless of how it comes to us, we can know the guidance is from our Higher Power if it promotes our good, seems positive and caring, and does not blame us or shame us.

Our responsibility is to use what guidance, support, and resources we receive. Our role is to take action.

Depending on the severity of our mental illness, we may not have sufficiently sound judgment—especially in the early stages of our dual recovery—to determine whether the guidance we perceive is coming from our Higher Power or from distorted thinking. If this is the case, it is wise to check frequently with others we trust who are in dual recovery about the validity of the guidance we receive.

The tools to help us

The power to decide

Although we are powerlessness over having our dual disorders, we are not hopeless. We still have the ability to decide how to manage the illnesses. Step Three is simply about making a decision. Some of us decide in a single moment of great inspiration to surrender to our Higher Power for good. But most of us don't have such remarkable experiences as we begin. Instead we need to make the decision each time we are faced with a new challenge or new opportunity. Change takes time. We proceed as we are guided to do, letting go of our old ways, only to find ourselves slipping back into them before long. We make the decision again, as many times as necessary, until the new way becomes a habit.

Trust

We practice trust—trust in our Higher Power, in those who have our best interests at heart, and in our own inner wisdom. Some of us have had so many frightening experiences and so many disappointments, we are reluctant to trust. We must regain this valuable skill or learn it for the first time.

Trust means putting our belief into action. We may have to start with the action first, knowing it is in our best interests. The trust will come later as we see the positive results.

Our resource pool

Some of us find that our Higher Power works through the people and circumstances of our lives, so we pay attention to what is going on around us and what people are saying. We use all the resources available that can contribute to a better life for us—healing treatments, competent and loving people, and day-by-day opportunities that come up.

If the nature of our psychiatric illness is such that we become severely impaired at times, we may have to ask someone to care for us totally. We may even have to authorize our caregivers to sign us into the hospital. This requires humility, but it is a way to make sure we are taken care of when we need to be. That is an important part of our recovery.

Barriers to overcome
Rejection of religion and God

Even after choosing a Higher Power in Step Two, we may still feel hesitant because of past problems with religion and God. If the feeling lingers, don't fight it. Recognize that choosing a Higher Power of your understanding is a new experience, and you need time to adjust to it.

Fear of loss of free will

When we first hear the suggestion that we turn our will and our lives over to our Higher Power, we might assume this means a complete loss of power for ourselves. Of course, none of us want to give up our self-determination. We want to be in control of our lives. Yet in the past we gave our will and our lives over to our drugs and our psychiatric illness. We became powerless over them.

Step Three is a chance to restore our inner power and achieve a balanced life by drawing on other sources of help—driving the Jaguar instead of the junker. We use our free will to choose our own Higher Power, one that we know is looking out for our best interests. Maybe we have chosen our recovery group or the Twelve Steps themselves as our Higher Power. Whatever we select as our source of help, we choose at every moment whether to respond to the guidance of this Helping Power. In doing so, we become free.

Uncertainty about how to "turn it over"

We may think we won't really know how to do this Step, how to surrender to a Higher Power. Yet we easily knew how to surrender to our drugs. We had an urge and we followed it. We showed little concern as we put alcohol and other drugs into our bodies, altering the delicate chemical balance in our brains. Most of us were well aware of the risks involved.

With Step Three, we plant a new urge in ourselves. We point ourselves in the direction of our Higher Power and use the tools of Step Three to keep moving in that direction. We learn how to do this through practice and through observing the experience of others.

Benefits
Sense of direction

We have set goals for ourselves and we now have a source of help to pursue them. We are growing in our belief that we will be steered back on course or redirected as needed.

Confidence

When we know we are no longer alone, when we have a sense of direction, we begin to feel better about ourselves. At first we feel a little insecure. We may just go through the motions, practicing these foundation Steps. But little by little, like an athlete doing daily push-ups and sit-ups, we feel stronger and stronger. We start to believe more in the program and in ourselves. We find that deciding to trust in our Higher Power was a wise choice. After all, it was our choice, whether our focus was on spirituality; good, organized direction; medical support; or some other source of help. Step Two asks us to choose it, Step Three encourages us to use it. Why? To put us more in touch with reality, so we don't make the same mistakes as much anymore. We start to feel better, look better, act better.

Stepping forward

The first three Steps build a foundation for recovery. They move us from a sense of deep failure, from feeling stuck, to a place of rebuilding. We find a new sense of motivation within ourselves. Having examined our powerlessness and our insanity, we now have committed ourselves to a new course of action—relying on a Higher Power to move us into a more promising future.

In Steps Four through Nine, we will discover how to make

this promise of a better future a reality. We begin Step Four the same way we might begin to look at what kind of job we might be able to do. We look at our assets and liabilities: the things that will help us in our recovery and the things that put us at risk for relapse.

STEP FOUR

Made a searching and fearless personal inventory of ourselves.

An *inventory* is simply an opportunity to study one's life and see it from a new point of view. In Step Four, we do an inventory to examine what helps our recovery and what hurts it—our assets and liabilities. Ordinarily in a Twelve Step program, we would start by focusing on liabilities so that we could first address what is hurting us. But in dual recovery, many of us begin by examining assets because we need extra strength to face honestly and courageously the areas of our lives that are causing us pain. We examine both our internal and external assets. To look at our internal assets, we identify and put in writing our beliefs, feelings, attitudes, and actions that can help us recover. We add to this list the external support we have available from professionals, family, other personal caregivers, medication, and other forms of treatment.

We also need to learn what may put us at risk for relapse. In our inventory, we identify and list any self-defeating and self-destructive beliefs, feelings, attitudes, and actions. These ways of hurting ourselves are liabilities. We also look at how we have hurt others, because the guilt, shame, and trauma that we feel about these experiences can interfere with our recovery. In addition, we want to be prepared to take responsibility for righting any wrongs to others, which we will do later in Step Nine.

Why Step Four is needed
We are unaware of our assets
If we know what strengths and resources we have to work with, we will know better how to carry out our recovery. We want to strengthen and increase our assets and decrease our liabilities. Many of us have thought we did not have any assets. We felt

like failures. We may have felt that we were so impaired by the symptoms of our psychiatric illness and our addiction that we could hardly lift our heads at times. Yet through our inventory, we gradually recognize what assets we have, and we are pleasantly surprised. We find that we have acquired quite a range of skills and developed many positive qualities. We begin to recognize the healthy relationships we have, our willingness to keep trying to get better despite devastating setbacks, and the times we have remained clean and sober. These are only a few examples. As we discover our assets, whether few or many, current or past, we know that we need never give up on ourselves. We see that we have enough, more than enough, to get started on dual recovery.

Our focus has been on the negative

Most of us have been bogged down in the problems of our dual disorders for a long time. We have been wrapped up in our symptoms, our recurring urge to drink or use, and the consequences and problems that result. Step Four helps us focus on solutions in a specific and concrete way: What have I got to work with? What needs changing? What do I have to clean up before I can move on? In the process of examining our assets and liabilities, we begin to see our recovery needs more clearly. Plans for recovery start to become apparent.

How Step Four works

Those of us severely impaired by a psychiatric illness can take a simple and concrete approach to Step Four. We examine the most basic of our assets and liabilities—how well we are taking care of our present daily needs. Many of us have difficulty managing basic tasks, such as obtaining food and shelter and simply being with other people. In a Fourth Step inventory, we look at our assets, the things we are able to do that work for us, the things that keep us healthy and promote stability. We also look at our liabilities, the things we do that are not working for us.

One way to do an inventory is to create and fill out a worksheet like the one on the next page, adding as many lines as you need for each topic. For each major area of need, make a list of your assets in the left-hand column and list your liabilities in the right-hand column.

What I need to do in my life

Things I can do that work for me		*Things I do that don't work for me*
_____	Don't drink or use drugs	_____
_____	Manage psychiatric symptoms	_____
_____	Get proper rest	_____
_____	Manage food, shelter, money	_____
_____	Be with people	_____
_____	Have fun	_____
_____	Cope with stress	_____
_____	Cooperate with case manager	_____
_____	Manage work, develop skills	_____
_____	Manage transportation	_____

❧

You can adapt the inventory to your individual ability, depending on the severity of your symptoms. Recognize that recovery may be very gradual, and that it may be months or years before you do a more in-depth inventory.

But when you become ready, do a Fourth Step inventory that examines in detail the issues presented by both illnesses. One way to do this inventory is to examine assets and liabilities in four areas:

1. *Symptoms* of both chemical dependency and emotional or psychiatric illness, and (for some) symptoms of multiple disorders.

2. *Values* that define how we view ourselves and our role in the world—in other words, a personal rulebook for living, will to live, or spiritual values.
3. *Beliefs, emotions, and behaviors*—day-to-day thoughts, feelings, and actions, including especially sensitive "hot spots" such as memories of past trauma.
4. *Relationships* with family, intimate partners, friends, caregivers, and acquaintances.

We look at the patterns of our symptoms

The symptoms of our dual disorders are unique to each of us. So are the ways we react to them. In an inventory, we look for the patterns both in our symptoms and in how we respond to them. We describe these patterns in writing and do our best to determine which are assets and which are liabilities. We also include any specific damage that has been done. We will use this damage list when we work Steps Eight and Nine. To do an inventory of our symptoms, we might ask ourselves these questions:

- Do the symptoms seem to come and go on their own?
- Are they worse at certain times?
- Are there times when I am free of symptoms?
- Do I experience some symptoms all of the time?
- Do these symptoms interfere with my ability to function and relate to others?
- How do I respond to symptoms? Do I panic? Give up? Avoid work, school, or family? Condemn myself? Reach out for help?
- What types of treatment have helped me manage symptoms?
- What appears to influence the onset of psychiatric symptoms?
- What appears to influence a relapse to using alcohol or other drugs?

We consider the complications of multiple disorders

Some of us have additional disorders and impairments, such as learning disabilities, head or spinal injuries, seizure disorders, vision and hearing impairments, or terminal illness. These are but a few examples. In reviewing symptoms, take into account the complications caused by having multiple disorders:

- Do the symptoms of the additional condition intensify the symptoms of my dual disorders?
- Have I received a good evaluation for my additional condition?
- Is the additional condition being properly treated and managed?
- Have I learned to cope in healthy ways with the additional condition?
- Has chronic (or terminal) illness interfered with my ability to function independently and have full use of my mind and body?

Note the liabilities caused by these complications, but be careful to list also the many personal assets that help you deal with your symptoms. You can call on your ability to learn, to communicate, and to accept life and live it to the fullest regardless of your condition and its limitations. Also acknowledge any other assets you have available, including the resources of the dual recovery program, plus a variety of medical and community resources.

Also list any specific damage caused by your symptoms. Ask yourself, Have I deteriorated physically? Have my symptoms caused a hardship for those around me? Have they caused me to neglect responsibilities?

We look at our values

We may call this an inventory of our inner self, our will to live, or our spiritual qualities. We look within ourselves and write a description of the values we find. We may ask ourselves questions such as, What do I believe about myself and the world I live in? Do I believe in a universal creator, a universal plan? How do I fit in? Do I believe the world is basically good, even though bad things have happened? Do I see all people as equal and worthy of respect? Do I respect myself? Have I lived by these values or have my dual disorders caused me to live in conflict with them?

We examine our beliefs, emotions, and behaviors

Our beliefs, emotions, and behaviors provide a source of strength for recovery, as well as the potential for relapse. Our *beliefs* about day-to-day events include expectations, assumptions, and opinions about everything from the way people treat us to how our bodies perform. In our inventory, we examine what we believe: Do I think having our dual disorders is unfair? Do I expect others to be responsible for my care? Do I assume the worst when symptoms appear or do I keep a positive outlook? Do I have a sense of humor about my condition? Do I fail to take it seriously? These are some of the questions we can ask ourselves to discover our liabilities and assets regarding our beliefs.

Some of our *emotions* may be liabilities when they place us at risk for relapse. Emotions such as anger, resentment, grief, anxiety, fear, guilt, shame, self-pity, and distorted self-image (inflated or poor) can put us at risk. But some of these same emotions can also be assets. Anger, for example, may help us take action when we need to draw the line on abuse. Joy, love, and compassion are a few other emotions we may list as assets.

Our *behavior* can certainly place us at risk. We may act without thinking. We may repeat certain harmful behaviors again and again. We may withdraw or become aggressive. We may continually criticize or ridicule ourselves or others. We may lie, cheat, steal, manipulate, neglect, ignore, threaten, assault, even kill. We may accept the abusive behavior of others. When we do an inventory, we list such behaviors as liabilities, including any damage we have caused. We also look to see what positive behaviors we exhibit or plan to develop that will help in our recovery—perhaps generosity, playfulness, creativity, or efforts to improve ourselves.

We look closely at our relationships

Our relationships are affected in many ways by our dual disorders. The effects are emotional, physical, financial, social, and spiritual. When our psychiatric symptoms are severe or when we are under the influence of intoxicating drugs, we may directly hurt people around us. In an inventory, we examine how we have affected others and what that has done to our relationships: Have I hurt someone's feelings? Have I disappointed people again and again with empty promises? Have I physically harmed someone? Have my illnesses created financial burdens for others? Have I shut myself off from others? Have I failed to appreciate important people in my life? Have I been pushy and overbearing?

Trying to hide the truth from others close to us and denying our disorders significantly affect these relationships. Excuses, blaming, and avoidance behavior may have alienated our loved ones and others we are responsible to. We have lost trust, and we have had difficulty solving problems and communicating with others.

Our assets are important to consider too. Ask, What am I doing well in terms of managing my symptoms? In what ways am I loving and responsible? What have I done to help others unselfishly despite having symptoms? What new efforts at honest communication am I now making? What good relationships do I have?

The tools to help us

Inventory worksheet

One way to write an inventory is to create worksheets for each of the four topic areas—symptoms (of each illness); values; beliefs, emotions, and behaviors; and relationships. You can list your assets and liabilities in two columns under each topic. For example:

Topic: Symptoms of chemical dependency

Assets	*Liabilities*
_____	_____
_____	_____

_____   _____

_____   _____

❧

You may wish to match specific assets with specific liabilities. For example, you might discover that your playful nature could help reduce controlling behavior by helping you lighten up and be less demanding. You can put the asset "playful nature" across from the liability "controlling behavior."

Be thorough with your inventory. Use as many sheets of paper as necessary to write a complete description of what you have to work with in your recovery. If your dual illnesses make it difficult for you to complete Step Four in writing, ask another person in recovery to help you with the writing. Speaking into a tape recorder is another way to record your inventory.

Barriers to overcome

Fear

Step Four asks us to make a searching and "fearless" inventory. Yet the idea of self-examination may scare us. What if we don't find any assets? What if what we learn about ourselves is too painful, disgusting, or overwhelming? What if we can't stand the thought of going over past problems again and want to avoid feelings of panic and anxiety?

Fears are all based on what-ifs rather than what is. We expect something terrible to happen. We worry that looking at the painful aspects of our lives will make the pain worse or make us relive it.

An inventory is simply an opportunity to study your life and see it from a new point of view. Be careful not to use the inventory to judge yourself as good or bad or to relive past grief, trauma, loss, pain, or shame. Rather, look to see what is working well and what helps, and what could put your recovery at risk. We are hunting for the truth about ourselves. The closer we get to our truth, the closer we get to sanity—living a life based on sound beliefs and actions. We recognize and accept our fears as we work Step Four, but nevertheless, because we trust the help of our Higher Power and the program, we proceed. Considering the alternative to recovery, which future do we really have the most to fear from?

Lack of organization

The idea of conducting a thorough, searching inventory may seem overwhelming. How can we ever explore all the aspects of our lives? How and when do we even begin? Some of us rush in and try to do too much, too quickly.

To do an inventory in an orderly and calm way, work with your source of help, sponsor, and group members. Do one thing at a time, in a simple, organized way. Write as much as you can at one time, perhaps a little each day. You may use the inventory guides in this chapter or some other Fourth Step guide that fits your needs.

You do not have to examine every aspect of your life with each inventory. Perhaps you can begin with your areas of highest risk for relapse. At a later time, you can do another inventory covering other areas. Special-topic inventories can be very useful in developing a quality recovery.

Denial

We may not always be comfortable with the way things are going, but the way we have been doing things feels familiar at least. We resist the idea of having to change anything. We don't want to acknowledge that we may have been acting in self-defeating and self-destructive ways. We may not even want to acknowledge our assets. Denial is an automatic self-protection system, a "watchdog." If we don't notice, we can get into a rut. But do we really want to stay in that painful, life-threatening rut? Step Four can lead us from an experience of deep pain to the experience of genuine freedom that comes from knowing the truth.

Sometimes we aren't sure if we are in denial about certain situations from our past. Because of the mental confusion that comes with our emotional or psychiatric illness or because of blackouts, we may not remember some or all of what happened in a particular incident. To help us deal this uncertain situation, we can ask any loving, caring people who were present at the time to describe what they remember about it. They may be able to help us get to the truth. If we have no way of knowing what actually happened, we can turn the matter over to our Higher Power, discuss it with our sponsor, and follow the guidance we receive. We may simply have to let go of some situations.

Benefits
An end to feeling broken

As we work Step Four, we gradually experience more and more stability. We are rebuilding what was broken, or at least had felt broken. We felt as if we had crumbled inside, or snapped. No more. Step Four helps us get ourselves back together.

As we discover our assets and liabilities and see ourselves in a new light, we may find that the damage we feel, though serious, is repairable. The pain, though severe, is not permanent. Perhaps we are just out of practice in some areas of our lives. Our many worthwhile assets (personal qualities, skills, and resources) have gone unused because we have directed so much of our time and energy toward the problems of our dual disorders. In many cases, it's not so much that we can't express ourselves, relate to others, or work at a job; we just haven't done it for awhile, or we haven't been able to develop that particular skill yet. Step Four is a way to examine our emotional, mental, and spiritual wounds and to tend them so we can begin to heal in a proper and practical way. We give ourselves a fresh start.

Clearer understanding of ourselves

Step Four gives us a clear view of who we are and where we are going. The once-fuzzy picture on the screen becomes clear. The interference goes away. We begin to see how and why we believe, feel, relate, and respond the way we do. We get an honest perspective on our lives. The pieces fit together better.

From this new self-knowledge comes a sense of strength, hope, and direction. Stress and anxiety are reduced as we understand better what is going on within us. We realize we have less to fear than we thought. We find we have more assets to help us than we knew. We see more clearly where the problems are coming from and what we can do about them. We feel more secure.

Stepping forward

Now that we have gathered all the information we can about our assets, our liabilities, and the damage we have caused, we can act on what we found. In Step Five, our first action is to admit what we have discovered, not only to ourselves, but to another person and our Higher Power. Sharing what we have learned about ourselves gives us the opportunity to confirm our new self-knowledge, connect deeply with it, clarify it further, and be empowered by it.

STEP FIVE

Admitted to our Higher Power, to ourselves, and to another human being, the exact nature of our liabilities and our assets.

So far our inventory has consisted of putting our memories, feelings, and ideas on paper. In Step Five, we use what we have written to acknowledge more deeply how our dual illnesses have affected ourselves and others. We share our inventory aloud with one other person and with our source of help. We no longer hang on to our secrets. Step Five puts us firmly in charge of our recovery.

With Step Five, we take a big step toward rejoining the human race. We go beyond the inner work of the first four Steps and reach out in a special way to at least one other person. For many of us, this may be a new experience. It may be the first time we have reached out with honesty and humility to begin rebuilding our connection with others.

Why Step Five is needed
We need total honesty

Alone, we may feel too frightened and overwhelmed to look at ourselves and our needs for recovery in an objective way. Telling our story to another person can make it easier to do so—especially if the person we choose to hear our Fifth Step is someone we admire and trust. If we are serious about recovery, we will do our best to tell the whole truth. The risks of relapse are too great if we live with lies, half-truths, or fuzzy uncertainty. By getting our assets and liabilities out in the open, we find it easier to own them, let go of the garbage, and move on.

We need to keep in mind that memories of events which occurred during episodes of our psychiatric illness and our intoxication may be inaccurate or unclear. The longer we are in recovery, the more we may recall. We may find it helpful to do additional Fourth and Fifth Steps as more information becomes available to us.

We have blind spots

Talking over our Fourth Step with another person can help us get past our blind spots and see the whole picture. Perhaps we do not like some aspect of ourselves. A Fifth Step listener may offer a more positive perspective on it. Maybe we are being grandiose, claiming no wrong on our part and blaming everyone else for our problems. Our listener may remind us to take a more honest, responsible look at our situation.

How Step Five works

We admit to ourselves

After we have completed writing our inventory, we ask ourselves: Have I been completely honest? Have I been searching and fearless? If we are satisfied that our inventory was thorough, we take some time to reflect on what we have written: What did I feel and experience as I did my inventory? What patterns of behavior did I see? What beliefs did I recognize that I was unaware of before? How have I been protecting myself in self-defeating ways? If we have kept a journal, we may find it useful to review what we have written there about our inventory.

In a self-loving way, we review all that we have discovered and accept that this is who we are right now. We try to forgive ourselves for any wrongs we have done. We recognize that we have done the best we could with what we understood and what we had to work with. After all, look at what we've been up against! But we know we have some work to do to complete our recovery process, and we admit that too.

We admit to our Higher Power

If we think of our Higher Power as having spiritual qualities, we quiet ourself, turn within, and reveal our discoveries. We set aside any fears we have about being judged or condemned. Knowing that our a Higher Power is truly a Helping Power, we look for a positive, caring response—acceptance, forgiveness. We find relief, knowing we are cleaning up our past and making a fresh start. We have a sense of gratitude, knowing that we have within us all the ability and strength we need for recovery.

If we have chosen another source of help as our Higher Power, we look for the right opportunity to share our inventory. If our Higher Power includes several people, such as a sponsor, a counselor, and our medical team, we ask one of them to hear our Fifth Step and we go over the same points. We inform the others that we are doing so, and we may decide to share some of our major insights with them as well. As we review the inventory, we look to see how the liabilities are out of sync with our concept of our Higher Power and how the assets are in sync with it. We can use a Fifth Step to recommit to working with our Higher Power to help us shape our lives.

We admit to another person

As soon as we complete our Fourth Step, we set up a time to do our Fifth Step with someone we trust and respect. We want to do this as soon as possible. We make every effort in meeting with this person to be honest and straightforward. We have nothing to lose by telling the truth, and a great deal to gain. We begin by explaining what we expect to get out of the meeting. We describe what we are going to do. Then we go over what we have written on paper.

Here's what we cover:

- the exact nature of our dual disorders and our symptoms, including any complications from multiple disorders
- our core spiritual values
- our beliefs, emotions, and behaviors
- our relationships
- our strengths and assets that we will build on in dual recovery
- the risks we face that may cause us difficulty in our dual recovery
- the damage our two illnesses has caused

We discuss what stood out for us as we wrote each item down and how we feel about it. We explain our "hot spots"—any painful or traumatic events that have affected our lives. If our emotional illness causes limitations or a permanent disability, we discuss this realistically. Developing any illness or condition that requires us to make major adjustments in our lives can seem unfair. The inconvenience of scheduling and going to a host of medical appointments, the financial burdens of the illness, and the demands of the treatment regimen, including taking medications, can seem overwhelming. We may resent the unfairness of it and be sad over the losses. We talk this over during our Fifth Step.

If we are looking for a specific type of feedback, we ask for it. The listener may help us sort out any unclear areas. Perhaps an episode of depression or manic behavior hurt the people around us. If we are uncertain how responsible we are for what happened, we ask for help in sorting this out. We do not expect our Fifth Step to be a therapy session, however. If we uncover especially troubling difficulties, we may want to seek professional help at a later time.

The tools to help us
The right person

Picking the right person to hear our Fifth Step is important. Some of us seek out a professional, such as member of the clergy, who is trained to hear a Fifth Step. Some of us choose a sponsor or another person who has been working a strong program and who demonstrates significant progress in dual recovery. Ideally, the person hearing our Fifth Step should be experienced in the Twelve Steps through personal recovery or be very familiar with the Twelve Steps, perhaps from experience as a caregiver. Others in recovery may be able to suggest someone they have found to be a good Fifth Step listener.

Most important is our attitude toward and opinion about the person. Are we comfortable with this person? Does he or she appear to be a good listener? Does he or she treat people well? If this person is recovering, do we admire his or her qualities of recovery? Does this person seem trustworthy? It is important to find someone who will listen attentively without judging us. We look for someone who will accept us, especially when we discuss our weaknesses. We need someone who can be encouraging in a sincere way. We do not expect the person to have any answers for us. It is important that the person agree to keep our conversation confidential.

The right time

Considering our emotional illness, we have to use good judgment to determine the best time to do our Fifth Step. We ask ourselves how emotionally ready we are to do it. Are we stable?

A Fifth Step should always be done in a self-loving way. We do not want to be brutal with ourselves. We do not want to open up old wounds without making sure we have the support we need to deal with them. If we find ourselves feeling too frightened or overwhelmed, we slow down and take a step back. We reflect on our assets. We talk over the process with our sponsor or a therapist. We proceed gently. If we are experiencing a serious episode of our psychiatric illness, it is best to wait until we are stabilized before going ahead with this Step. Yet we do not wait too long. We take advantage of the benefits of this Step as soon as possible, a time best determined in consultation with our therapist and sponsor.

Barriers to overcome

Procrastination

It's so easy to wait. There are a hundred excuses why now is not the time to do a Fifth Step. But recovery can't wait. Are we willing to risk relapse? We have three choices: we can go backwards, we can stay stuck, or we can step further into freedom.

Oddly enough, sometimes doing a good Fourth Step can create the risk of feeling too good. We may experience a great deal of inner strength and clarity and relief from much of our emotional pain. We may think we have gone far enough in dual recovery and do not need the rest of the Steps. But the truth is, we have only begun to experience the power and joy of recovery. Yes, it can get even better. But on the flip side, if we are not careful, we risk losing our good feelings of the moment and slipping backward in our recovery. Even though we have recognized our liabilities in Step Four, we have not yet taken the steps that lead to the kind of in-depth change needed for long-term dual recovery. Step Five starts us on that course.

Fear

By nature, we tend to protect ourselves from pain and threats and to move toward pleasure and self-interest. If we believe doing a Fifth Step is too great a threat, this natural sense of self-protection may kick in. We will think of many reasons to avoid it.

- I might experience pain, shame or guilt.
- I will lose control.
- I will be judged.
- Why bother? It's stupid.
- Why bother? It won't help. I've failed at everything else.
- The person hearing my Fifth Step won't understand.
- My confidentiality may be broken.
- I've quit drinking and taking drugs, and I'm taking medications to manage my symptoms. I don't see any reason to change anything else.

Fear, no matter what form it takes, can paralyze us, keeping us stuck in our old ways of coping. With the help of our sponsor and our Higher Power, we can look realistically at each of our fears and go beyond them. We discover our fears are unfounded or exaggerated. If necessary, we do more work on Step Three and Step Four to understand our fears better and turn them over to our Higher Power. When we feel certain that discomfort or other problems might arise from doing a Fifth Step, we do what we can to lessen them, but then we go ahead with it.

Benefits

Relief and healing

If we have been thorough in our Fourth Step inventory and honest in our Fifth Step, sooner or later we experience a sense of relief. For some of us, the Fifth Step is a moving, spiritual experience. Others simply have a sense of completing a necessary task. Whether or not we have any special emotional reaction, we find that over time the quality of our recovery is improving. The healing we came to believe in in Step Two starts becoming concrete. We no longer have to repeat our mistakes because we are now aware of them.

Acceptance and forgiveness

When someone listens to our story and says "I understand," it may be the first time we have heard those words. We don't feel so alone anymore. A listener may tell us he or she had similar experiences in the past, yet is now experiencing recovery. Maybe there is hope for us! We find it easier to stop feeling ashamed of ourselves. We can begin to accept ourselves just as we are. We admit our assets and liabilities to ourselves, to our Higher Power, and to another human being, in part because we are so hungry for acceptance and forgiveness. We want to feel equal again. In Step Five, we find that despite all the misery and difficulty we and others have experienced as a result of our dual disorders, we are good people who are still okay.

A new perspective

As we describe our circumstances to another person, we get a new perspective on them, a new point of view. Somehow, as we say these things aloud, they sound different. Some of them may not seem as terrible as we thought. Others that we thought were unimportant may suddenly seem very significant. In addition, the other person may relate to what we say and describe how he or she handled a similar circumstance. This may give us some new ideas.

A clearer focus

Step Five brings our recovery plan out of our heads, off the paper, and into our daily life with other people. We find it easier to understand and follow the plan for recovery and to use the tools that are available to help us. More and more, we move from a victim position to a recovery position. We have shared and celebrated our assets with another. Our self-esteem is raised. We are better able to distinguish ourselves from our illnesses. We can say, Yes, this is the history of my symptoms and the problems they created for me and others, but this history does not make me a bad person. We recognize that we are responsible for our recovery and we feel good about it. We are more confident, capable, and ready to move ahead.

Stepping forward

We have done our homework. We have a good understanding of our situation, we trust that recovery is possible for us, and we have told someone else the whole truth about ourselves. At this point, we can hardly help but move forward. Yet we are at another decision point. Like the patient who has the full lab report on a physical condition, we have the full report on our spiritual condition. Now we are at the point of deciding what to do about it. Will we make a commitment to continue down the path of recovery? It only makes sense to do so, despite any fears or misgivings we may have. Yet it is our choice. Step Six helps us make that commitment to follow the treatment plan for our dual disorders.

STEP SIX

Were entirely ready to have our Higher Power remove all our liabilities.

In Step Six, we make a commitment to use our chosen source of help to aid us in letting go of what is hurting us. We have examined and acknowledged both our assets and liabilities in Steps Four and Five. We found that the liabilities interfered with our ability to manage our dual disorders. Now we decide to give up the liabilities. We are ready to let go of the pain, and the beliefs and behaviors that contribute to it.

To give up our old way of doing things takes attention and effort. We're used to the way we've always done things, and we may believe that change is too hard. Step Six offers time to pause and consider, Am I willing to get well? Am I willing to do whatever it takes? We are reminded in this Step that we have all the resources of our Higher Power available to help us. But it is up to us to make the choice to accept the help. We prepare ourselves to get well.

Why Step Six is needed
Change doesn't come quickly

Steps Six and Seven are often seen as combination Steps. You might wonder why Step Six is necessary at all. Why not jump right into Step Seven and get busy with the changes that need to be made? For the same reason we don't just jump into our car and take off when we are ready to make a long trip—we need to plan our itinerary, pack the bags, check the tires, and fill the gas tank.

In the same way, going off in a new direction in one's life takes some preparation. We will be driving down some unfamiliar roads, facing different conditions, perhaps meeting some new roadblocks. It takes great courage and strength to face these new challenges. Doing things the old, familiar ways always seems so much easier. But if we want recovery, we need a change of attitude and action. If we thought our only hope for enjoying life was to get high, we have to become willing to seek others ways to enjoy life. If we expect quick fixes for our illnesses, we have to be willing to learn patience and persistence (perhaps trying several therapies or medications before we find one that works for us).

Change takes time, attention, determination, and openness to guidance from our source of help. To get rid of old pain and current pain, we may temporarily have to experience a new kind of pain—growing pain. But haven't we experienced enough pain already? We have indeed known deep pain from the effects of our illnesses. But this new pain is not another result of our illnesses. Rather, this pain moves us down the path of recovery. It is a way of continuing the healing within us and within our relationships.

How Step Six works
We decide to trust

Crossing a creek in the woods can be a delightful adventure when you are out walking with friends. Spotting a rock in the middle, you know you can get across if you help each other out. You hold the hand of someone behind you while you steady yourself, reaching your foot out onto the rock. Then, at the critical moment, you make a decision of trust. You let go of the person's hand, shift your balance forward onto the rock. You trust that as you reach out your other foot, you will successfully land on the other side of the creek and you won't slip and fall.

Step Six is like that moment of decision. With the helping hand of our Higher Power, we get started; we step out and steady ourselves, and then we prepare to go forward. We trust that we'll make it to the other side. We trust that the support we need will be awaiting us there. We let go and take hold

Step Six means letting go so we can take hold. We review what we have done in the first five Steps and decide if we're ready for the new life offered in dual recovery. Being ready involves a clear decision, a commitment. We may make the decision in a quiet moment of reflection. The decision may be the result of gentle prodding from a sponsor or counselor. It may come when someone we trust confronts us and makes clear to us how much damage we are doing to ourselves or to others. We may even reach our decision when life becomes so unpleasant we can't bear to repeat the past. For some of us, it takes frequent relapses to prompt our commitment.

If we have done our homework in the first five Steps, Step Six will seem like a natural thing to do. Why on earth would we want to hang on to a life of unmanageability that has caused us and others so much distress? We have already faced our desperation in Step One; developed a vision of recovery for ourselves and identified a source of help in Step Two; decided to open up to positive, caring guidance in Step Three; and learned what we had to work with in Steps Four and Five. To move toward our vision, we have now only to decide to make the necessary changes. And every time we get careless and return to our old ways, we will need to make the decision again. Step Six helps us make and maintain constructive change.

The tools to help us

Serenity Prayer

To make the changes that will lead us toward our vision of recovery, we need courage and wisdom. We also need faith and peace to accept the circumstances in our lives that we cannot change. The Serenity Prayer expresses our desire for the help we need. For some, it becomes a philosophy of life.

> *God, grant me the serenity*
> *To accept the things I cannot change,*
> *The courage to change the things I can,*
> *And the wisdom to know the difference.*

If the concept of God or spirituality is not part of our beliefs, we turn for direction, courage, and serenity to whatever our chosen Higher Power is. We look to a good, organized direction, a plan we can follow to shape our lives in a way that builds us up and moves us forward.

Our will to live

Somewhere inside us, we have an inner spirit or will to survive that keeps us going, even in the toughest of times. We have a spark of belief in ourselves that has kept us from giving up on life. In fact, it has brought us to the point of wanting to do this Step so we can get well. The way to recovery may not be clear to us yet, but our spirit makes it possible to trust that the process will all make sense in due time.

This life-sustaining spirit is our number-one asset. It connects us with our creative energy and motivation. It prompts us to say, "Let's go for it." We can trust this spirit. We can use it. It will help us become ready to change.

The experience of others

Step Six is a special, personal experience. Each person comes to the point of being ready to change in a different way. Yet to discover our own way, we may benefit from hearing the experience of others. Others in recovery will be happy to share their experience, strength, and hope with us. By learning what helped them become more open to change, we find it easier to discover our own way of opening up.

Humility, honesty, and willingness

The ways we adapted to the symptoms and consequences of our dual disorders in the past seemed automatic. They fit with our beliefs. Yet we may not have been aware of our choices at the time. Gradually these ways of adapting became habits that felt very much a part of us. Now we recognize the need for leaving those habits behind, acknowledging that maybe they weren't such a good idea after all, or at least that they don't fit our beliefs or needs anymore. It takes honesty and humility to admit our mistakes, to change course. It also takes humility to accept the help of a Higher Power. We'd prefer to do it ourselves. Step Six, then, requires a willingness to set aside our arrogance and be open to new ideas.

Step Six

Barriers to overcome

"I can't"

We find lots of ways to avoid Step Six:

- I've tried to do things differently before and it didn't work.
- I can't right now. I'll do it later.
- I really don't care.
- I won't be able to face it if my partner walks out on me because I won't drink with her anymore.
- My friends on the street expect me to be there. I can't disappoint them.

When we are discouraged by so many failures in the past, sometimes it just seems as if we can't possibly make a new commitment to change. We're afraid to believe that things could turn out well. We're afraid of another disappointment. We also become fearful of change and what it will cost us. So we come up with a whole list of "I can'ts." We fail to believe in ourselves and our source of help.

If we find ourselves hesitating at Step Six, we go back to the previous Steps and see what we missed: Is my vision of dual recovery clear? Have I found a Higher Power I can trust? Does this Higher Power really make sense to me? Have I thoroughly identified my assets and do I really believe in them? Having answered these questions, we hold back no longer. We become ready to move ahead and pursue all the benefits of recovery.

We sometimes wonder why we should bother, since our illnesses will always be with us, producing some symptoms. If we believe we will never regain our old abilities and be like "normal" people, is recovery worth the effort? With Step Six, we go ahead and prepare to make whatever changes that we can make, accepting our limitations. Then we are patient with our progress. We do the best we can, and we know that is good enough. We may even discover that some of our lost abilities are replaced by new ones we have yet to imagine.

Inertia

Maybe we feel stuck. Just as we have trouble getting out of bed on a cold morning, we have a tough time getting going with the changes we know we need to make. That's called *inertia*. We keep doing things the way we have always done them because, well, it's a habit. But in this case, inertia might also mean staying with the pain and misery we want so much to get rid of. Talking about change and thinking about change won't make anything happen. Making a clear-cut decision in Step Six, after laying solid groundwork, will get us ready to move.

Benefits

An end to the confusion

Step Six is the point at which we make a definite commitment. We are no longer on the fence. We choose recovery wholeheartedly. We go from talk to action; we walk the walk. What a relief! Confusion and indecision can be so frustrating, so exhausting. Now we leave that behind. We move forward.

A new freedom

In making the decision, we open the way to reach a new level of freedom. We prepare to free ourselves from the liabilities that have held us back. We let go of the heavy load of our own making and take hold of a more manageable pack to carry—a pack filled with directions and supplies to take us down the road to recovery.

Stepping forward

Step Six gets us ready. We open our hearts and minds to change and to receive the help we need. We are prepared to change deeply because we want so much to recover from our dual disorders. We do not expect magical cures. We work toward daily progress in our recovery. In this state of readiness, we can approach Step Seven and ask with confidence for the help that we need.

Step Seven

*Humbly asked our Higher Power to remove these liabilities
and to help us to strengthen our assets for recovery.*

With inventory in hand and a willing spirit, we begin to
live a wholehearted commitment to recovery in Step
Seven. We take action to let go of the liabilities that have held
us back, and we take hold of our assets and put them to use.

Dual recovery is such a major change in our lives that we
turn to our Higher Power to take the lead. With an attitude of
humility, we rely on our source of help—whether a spiritual
source or some other source, such as our fellowship or the Steps
themselves—to shape our lives in a new way. Our purpose is
not to humiliate ourselves, but rather to recognize the truth
that we cannot change without help.

Why Step Seven is needed
We need to change

By the time we get to Step Seven, we see more clearly that we
do need to make changes in order to maintain recovery and
prevent relapse. Our usual way of doing things has not been
working for us. Unless we do something different, our situation
will stay the same or deteriorate.

We need help to change

Step Seven asks us to approach change with humility. Humility
is simply seeing and acknowledging the truth about ourselves,
our needs, and our direction. Humility is not new to us in Step
Seven. We use it in every stage of our recovery. Admitting our
powerlessness takes great humility. So do turning to a new
source of help and acknowledging our assets and liabilities.
Now, in Step Seven, we call on humility again to acknowledge
the need for help in changing our liabilities and making the
most of our assets. We ask for this help from our Higher Power.

How Step Seven works
We make the request

For those of us who choose a spiritual Higher Power, we simply turn to this Power in a time of prayer and ask for the help we need to make the necessary changes. By asking, we also make a commitment to a new way of doing things. Some of us do this eagerly because we recognize our recovery depends on it. Others may feel reluctant to change yet make the choice to move ahead with it. We make a commitment to let go of useless and harmful patterns of living. We commit to making the most of our assets.

If we have chosen another source of help as our Higher Power, we make the same request and the same commitment. If our Higher Power is a group, we ask for and welcome feedback in our meetings. If our Higher Power is a program; a plan we follow; or a good, organized direction, we step forward to accept the guidance we are given. (The asking is implied.) For example, if the Steps themselves are our source of help, studying them and following them closely becomes our way of seeking and using help to change our ways. The Steps become our source of courage, strength, and hope.

We ask for outside help at this point because by ourselves we have so much trouble changing our self-defeating and self-destructive attitudes and behaviors. We may even be blind to many of them. Although we did our best to examine them in both our Step One history and our Step Four inventory, we can't always get a good perspective on our own situation. Working with our Higher Power provides an objective view. For example, we may criticize ourselves for being impatient with others, but our Higher Power can help us see that a bigger problem is how impatient we are with ourselves over the slow progress we are making in dealing with our illness. We may discover that what we need to do is to begin changing our self-image and setting more reasonable expectations for ourselves. Once we do that, our expectations of others may gradually become more reasonable as well. Our Higher Power can also help us become more aware of our assets. We may be unaware because we think of ourselves as failures, unable to get well.

We act as if

Even when we can see the changes we need to make and genuinely want to make them, we might feel uncomfortable moving ahead with them. If we have always hung out with people who drink or use, we feel awkward trying to make new friends. If we have suffered traumatic abuse and neglect in the course of our emotional or psychiatric illness, trusting others can be extremely difficult. Yet as our liabilities are removed through Step Seven, we will no longer be comfortable with our old ways either. So, for a time, we will be in a state of change and feel unsure. Yet we are ready now to live a saner, healthier life. We recognize we have nothing to lose by trying out new beliefs and behavior.

To help us practice new behavior, we "act as if." To act as if means that we go ahead with the new behavior, despite our discomfort. We act as if we are already able to do it. We walk through the pain and fear. For instance, we might apply for a job despite self-doubts. We might start a friendship by asking someone from our meeting or our neighborhood to go out for pizza or to a movie. We might take extra time to dress well and make ourselves look attractive. If these are new or neglected activities for us, some initial awkwardness is normal, but we are surprised how quickly our confidence builds. We "act as if" because we want so badly to recover, and we find that, yes, we are recovering and it feels right and good. Once we change our behavior, our hearts, minds, and feelings usually follow.

We are patient with our progress

Step Seven can seem like a magical step; we expect that suddenly our liabilities will be removed and we will be a new person. It's true, we do have a new perspective if we are sincere in working Step Seven. But it will take lots of practice for our new behaviors to become habits. We need patience with our progress. We developed our liabilities over many years. We need some time to free ourselves from them and replace them with more helpful assets. We have also had some of our assets for many years, but we still need time to develop them.

The tools to help us
A journal

Keeping a written daily journal of our progress can offer encouragement as we face the challenging task of making changes. We sort out our feelings as we practice new behaviors. We celebrate each small step forward. In Step Ten, we will see the value of journaling and inventory again.

Commitment to others

Telling people we trust about our commitment to make changes can be a very useful tool. We will get support, encouragement, and reminders from them. We are also less likely to go back on a promise to change if we have said it aloud. Building healthy relationships is an added benefit.

Barriers to overcome
Fear of loss of control

If we always do things the same way, we become used to that way of doing things, and we can predict the results. Once we change the way we do something, however, suddenly the outcome is not so predictable. We may feel awkward, confused, out of control, scared. For example, the episodes of our psychiatric illness can follow a predictable pattern, so that even though we may feel "crazy," to some extent we know what to expect. As our symptoms become more manageable, however, life may seem more unpredictable. For instance, if we are used to keeping to ourselves, we find that being out among people makes us nervous. At first, we don't know how to act. We believe people are judging us, and we assume they are rejecting us. We feel out of control. Yet this feeling is only temporary. Gradually we learn to change our beliefs, expectations, and behavior through practice. We learn to relax. And we learn that we do not have to control what others think and do. As we ask for and accept help in Step Seven, we become more comfortable with a healthier way of doing things.

Fear of making a commitment to recovery

What if we tell someone we are going to do things differently and then goof up? What will that person think of us? How will we ever be able to hold our heads up? Fear of failure and the resulting shame can cause us to hesitate to make a commitment in the first place. But what is the cost if we don't do things in a saner way? Will we find ourselves slipping backward in our program? Will we stay stuck in the same old misery? Probably.

When we rely on the guidance of our chosen source of help, we can feel confident in making any needed changes. We can trust that despite any initial awkwardness and mistakes, we will succeed in the end. We use the tool of patience to help us try again. We also remember that the opinions of others are not our Higher Power. Rather, we follow the direction of the source of help we have chosen, and we trust in our own humility—which means seeing ourselves truthfully as good and worthwhile people.

Benefits

Changes in liabilities and assets

The most obvious benefit from Step Seven is that our liabilities are removed and our assets strengthened. How can we be sure this is happening?

- *We experience an obvious change in attitude and actions.* We will notice, or maybe others will notice first, that something in our attitude or actions has changed. Perhaps you used to throw a fit every time your roommate moved your keys, but now you find yourself feeling calmer in this situation. Where you used to assume your roommate was intentionally trying to annoy you, now you might respectfully ask your roommate to let you know before moving anything of yours. Or you might just pray the Serenity Prayer and let it go.
- *We experience a change in our illnesses.* We find ourselves less interested in drinking or using other drugs. We gladly and regularly avoid situations where we might be at risk. We also find a new inner strength that makes us better able to recognize and deal with our symptoms, to separate ourselves from our psychiatric illness, and to go from being victimized to being in charge of our recovery. Where we

had given up before, now we make an effort. Our bitterness gradually turns to acceptance and even willingness.

- *We experience spiritual insight.* A moment may come when we suddenly have no desire anymore for certain past ways of doing things. We have a spiritual experience that reminds us we are capable and worthy of having a better life. Our will to live becomes stronger. We have found a Power that has helped give our lives meaning.

Stepping forward

The changes we have made in Step Seven, in cooperation with our Higher Power, have mostly been within ourselves. Now, in Step Eight, we prepare to reach out to others and repair any damage that has been done as a result of our dual disorders.

STEP EIGHT

Made a list of all persons we had harmed and became willing to make amends to them all.

In Step Eight, we look to see who our illnesses have affected and prepare to heal and rebuild our relationships. We have suffered a great deal from our two illnesses. Others around us have suffered as well. There is a need for mending to take place within us and between us. In most cases, we did not intend to hurt anyone, including ourselves. But we and others have been hurt. In Step Eight, we make a list of the people who have been hurt. We become willing to do the best we can to tend to those hurts and make things right again.

Step Eight helps us confirm that we are not bad people, but good people with two serious illnesses. We are willing to take responsibility for our actions. If we were negligent in following our program of dual recovery and relapsed to our psychiatric symptoms or to using alcohol or other drugs, we accept responsibility for any resulting actions that caused harm. But in some cases, despite our best efforts to manage our psychiatric illness, the illness is so severe that we cannot control what we do. During an acute episode, we may have unintentionally injured someone—for example, while hallucinating and defending ourselves against a "devil." We do not consider ourselves fully responsible for such action, especially if we have done the best we can to manage our illness. Yet we may *feel* responsible, and we may want to make amends to the person we injured.

In Step Eight, we find a renewed sense of our morals and values. We want to heal any hurts from the past, not only out of shame and remorse, but because it is the right thing to do. We know we can't really go forward in recovery until we clean up the wreckage from the past. Step Eight is a solid Step that helps us accept our dual illnesses and also our responsibility for dual recovery.

Why Step Eight is needed

We are burdened by shame

We have felt very ashamed about our illnesses and about what we have done or been unable to do because of them. That shame has weighed us down. It altered our image of ourselves and fostered self-hate. We thought of ourselves as failures and bad people. With that view of ourselves, we had a difficult time believing we could do anything right. We felt that we deserved condemnation rather than friendship, bad things rather than good. We could not even fully accept the good that came our way, because we felt sure it was only a matter of time before things would go bad again.

To recover, we need to get rid of the shame. We need to change our view of ourselves. Step Eight is our opportunity to start mending the past so we can leave it behind us once and for all.

We rediscover our values

We are good people. We confirm that we have good values deep within us. But they may be distorted in our shame and self-hate. Step Eight prepares us to seek and grant forgiveness and to make up for the past. As we reconnect with our values of compassion, concern, and harmony, we will want to take these actions. We will want to see the damage that has been done and make every effort to repair it.

We examine our relationships

Steps One through Seven focused our attention on our inner development. Now we start to look outward. What shape are our relationships in?

Many of us have strained relations with important people in our lives. Parents, partners, other caregivers, children, and friends have all felt the effects of our illnesses. So have employers, co-workers, and others we have had close contact with. If we are honest with ourselves, we notice that we even have strained relations with ourselves. Haven't we failed to take care of ourselves through fear, defiance, or self-hate? Perhaps we even tried to end our own lives. Have we neglected to respect ourselves? Have we not adapted our lives to our chemical dependency and psychiatric illness rather than to a program of dual recovery? Step Eight is needed to get a clear understanding of the damage that has been in all our relationships. It is also needed to prepare the heart and mind to right the wrongs, mend our relationships, and heal our pain.

How Step Eight works
We make a list

If we were thorough in Step Four, we have a big jump on Step Eight. By reviewing what we discovered about our relationships in Step Four, we easily notice who we have harmed. Our main task in Step Eight is to make a list of these people.

By putting the list in writing, we go from feeling ashamed and helpless about each situation to seeing the possibility for healing. The list of names becomes part of our plan for recovery. It also becomes a commitment. Once we've written a name on the list, we won't take it off. We're committed to doing something about this strained relationship. We have a checklist for action.

If you are not quite clear about who to put on the list, go over once again how your illnesses and how you have dealt with them have affected you and the people around you. Ask yourself, Did I engage in illegal activity to obtain money for drugs? Did I lie about what I was doing, where I was going, how I got the money? Did my actions cause financial problems? Did I engage in aggressive and abusive behavior? Did I isolate myself and withdraw from others? Did I neglect my family, job, other responsibilities? Did my relationships fall into an unhealthy rut?

When I was suffering from psychiatric symptoms, did I create distress for those around me? Did I ignore them or blame them? Did I fail to appreciate their concern for me? Did I, in manic episodes, spend their money, jeopardize their security, or put them at risk in some way? Did I make promises I didn't keep? Did I, while depressed, hurt them or lie to them to get them to leave us alone?

What about the way I treated myself? Did I neglect my health? Did I constantly criticize myself?

Be thorough in reviewing any damage you have caused.

You can also ask yourself if you need to mend your relationship with your Higher Power: Has my behavior been at odds with my Higher Power? Have I followed a good, orderly direction? Did I disregard the natural order of things by putting harmful chemicals in my body, thus risking the life, health, and safety of myself and others?

You might hesitate to put some people on your list because you believe they are the ones at fault. But Step Eight asks us to examine our responsibility, however small, for any problems that have occurred. Did we try to get back at them? Did we hold on to resentments? Did we condemn them in our minds? If we want recovery, we cannot afford to hold ill will toward anyone. We must not only clear up the damage from our actions, but also work on any attitudes or thoughts that continue to undermine our peace of mind. Of course, we do not need to take on responsibility that is not ours. If others abused us or judged us harshly, we are not responsible, and we will want to consider the needs of our recovery carefully in dealing with these situations.

We evaluate our responsibility for our actions

What about the actions we took while under the influence of drugs or during episodes of our psychiatric illness? Do we make amends for those since we are not responsible for having these illnesses? To answer that question, we need to examine honestly our own experience with the help of our sponsor or others we respect in recovery. We review each situation and determine, as best we can, the extent of our responsibility for what happened. Failing to take prescribed medications, neglecting to have required blood tests done, and failing to report honestly how treatments are affecting us are examples of choices that could result in a return of psychiatric symptoms and continued harmful consequences for ourselves and others. Allowing ourselves to get overstressed and overtired, staying around people who prompt us to use alcohol or other drugs, and neglecting to get the support we need are a few of the ways that might lead us back to our addictive behaviors and the harmful actions that result. We need to consider seriously our values, attitudes, and behaviors in these situations to determine how responsible we are for what happened.

Perhaps more important is feeling responsible for whatever hurt our illnesses have caused. We are careful not to bury ourselves in shame, yet we do not want to deny our wrongdoings to avoid real feelings. The goal is to have a clear conscience and a fresh start in every way possible. We want to have a genuine concern for how others have been affected. Though parents are not directly responsible when their child accidentally breaks something during a visit to a friend's home, they still feel bad about what happened and should offer to repair or replace it. Likewise, we may not have intentionally hurt anyone, yet the people around us have suffered and we want to do what we can to heal that hurt.

We become willing to make amends

The second half of Step Eight helps us get our attitude ready for making amends. We have already made so much progress in the program. We are feeling stronger, more like a whole person. We have our feet on the ground. But we know there is still more to maintaining recovery and preventing relapse. We have not yet achieved as much peace of mind as we would like. Our relationships are improving, but we have a way to go. We want so much to make peace with the past; to have honest, caring relationships in the present; and to let go of our fears about the future. We have had a glimpse of the full benefits of recovery and are now willing to do even more to achieve them.

The tools to help us
Paper and pen

It sounds simple, but paper and pen are exactly what we need to move ahead with this Step. We write a list. We get the names out of our heads and onto paper. We get started with this phase of our recovery one name at a time.

Caring advisors

We may need a lot of help from others to complete this Step if we are hesitant or unsure. We can ask others at our meeting how they handle preparing a list and becoming willing. We attend Step Eight meetings to learn more. If we have trouble sorting out our responsibility in a particular relationship, a sponsor can be particularly helpful. We talk over the situation and ask for objective feedback. Certainly, we can turn to our Higher Power to help us become willing to make amends. Keep in mind that "becoming willing" is a process. Like all the Steps, it takes time. Take the time, use the tools, put in the effort, and the willingness comes.

Barriers to overcome

Fear

To some of us, the idea of making amends is frightening. We just can't imagine going to someone and expressing our feelings about the way we have hurt him or her. We are too embarrassed, too ashamed. We anticipate all kinds of terrible reactions from the other person and we become scared.

In Step Eight, we are not yet making the amends, only the preparations. We are not meeting anyone face to face yet, so we can let go of our fears and shame. We are simply making a list of names on paper, recalling what happened, and getting our hearts and minds ready for making amends. No one can react badly to us for doing that. We take this Step by itself before moving on to Step Nine, confident that if we prepare well for our amends, Step Nine will take care of itself.

Denial

We still may be experiencing denial in some areas of our lives. We blame others for the problems in our relationships and refuse to see our part. We can choose to stay with this outlook, but if we do, our recovery is in danger. We are still trying to change others instead of ourselves. Others are not the ones in need of our recovery. We are. If we continue to stay in denial and protect our feelings, what will be the price?

Unhealthy relationships

Of course, we may not want to have an ongoing relationship with some of the people we have harmed. They may have hurt us too much, or we may feel they could hamper our recovery. But that does not relieve us of the responsibility to make amends for any past harm done. If we are willing to make these amends, we can say goodbye to the relationship and all the associated blame and shame at the same time.

Benefits
A sense of being whole

Step Eight gives us directions for cleaning up our past and moving on. We no longer have to feel broken. We are mending ourselves and our relationships. Having stopped the unmanageable cycle of chaos caused by our dual disorders, we are prepared now to reconnect with the world around us in a healthy way. With courage and honesty, we accept responsibility for the consequences of our illnesses. We start to feel whole.

Higher self-esteem and self-image

More and more now, we are seeing ourselves as separate from our illnesses. We recognize that our illnesses have created problems, but we are not the problems. Because we are basically good, we are prepared to do what we can to correct the problems. We show concern for others and act responsibly. We are willing to get well.

Stepping forward

Now that we have identified the amends we need to make and have become willing to make them, we move into Step Nine. We do not hesitate out of fear or worry. Rather, we move ahead eagerly in order to complete our recovery goals.

Made direct amends to such people wherever possible, except when to do so would injure them or others.

Our purpose in Step Nine is to mend our relationships in a direct and meaningful way. In Step Eight, we decide what relationships need mending and we become willing to make the necessary amends. Step Nine is the action Step. We make every effort to go directly to the people who were hurt because of our dual disorders, we acknowledge the harm done, and we make changes or restitution to correct whatever situations we can. We make a fresh start.

Why Step Nine is needed

Our strained relations hurt us

If we feel responsible for hurting others, that can be a heavy burden on our minds. We feel guilty and ashamed, and our level of stress rises. We assume that people think badly of us. We may avoid the people who were hurt. We may miss out on an opportunity for a friendship or a job or some other advantage, because a barrier exists between us and the people we harmed. If what we did was hidden, we may worry about getting caught someday.

If we have hurt ourselves, we also feel bad. We wonder, How could I have let that happen to me? What's wrong with me?

If what we have done puts us at odds with our Higher Power, we also are disturbed. We feel off balance, out of harmony with life.

The more we become honest in recovery and come to understand our own feelings, the more we become aware of how others feel when we hurt them. We want to make sure we are living by the Golden Rule instead.

Step Nine is our chance to mend our relationships and our

lives. We unload the burdens of the past and prepare to go forward with a clear conscience.

We need strength for our recovery

Because of the difficulties of our illnesses, many of us have felt weak. We believed that we would panic if we tried to make amends. We doubted that we could go through with it. We may not have realized how much courage it has taken for us to get this far. Because we have thought of ourselves as weak, we may hold back. Our "courage muscles" have gotten a little flabby. We've been running scared.

Step Nine is an opportunity to exercise our inner strength and demonstrate our commitment to recover. We take a courageous stand. We contact the people affected by our illness. We mend the relationships through our words and our actions. At first we may feel awkward and uncomfortable, but like an athlete who practices over and over to build up strength and endurance, we take on this exercise of rebuilding relationships with vigor. We gradually develop the skills to maintain healthy relationships, which we seek so desperately in our recovery.

How Step Nine works
We make the amends

We take our list from Step Eight and set off on a new adventure. We may start with anyone on our list. Some of us find it helpful to approach the easiest amends first and build up courage to do the more difficult ones. Others want to get the more difficult ones over first. We each set our own priorities. Our sponsor can help.

Then we make our amends. One way to begin is by reviewing these questions before meeting with each person: What did I do and how did it affect this person? How did I feel about it then and how do I feel now?

Then proceed with making the amends in the following manner:.

- Whenever possible, set up a meeting with each person.
- You may wish to tell the people you are making amends to about your dual disorders.

- Explain that you are now following a program of dual recovery. Tell them you are managing your illnesses in a constructive way and you want to have a healthier relationship with them.
- Let them know how important it is for your recovery to talk with them about the way your illnesses have affected them.
- Express your regret for any harm you have caused them.
- Offer to do what you can to make things right.
- Make restitution as needed, or perform whatever service you can to ease the strain in the relationship.

We do not make our amends in a groveling or self-pitying way. We maintain our self-respect and sense of purpose. We set proper boundaries with people who could threaten our mental health, sobriety, or peace of mind. We simply make our amends to them, but we do not accept abusive or inappropriate behavior from them in the process. If we are concerned in any way about meeting someone, we arrange to meet in a safe place—perhaps at a restaurant or another public place. We may ask other supportive people to be present.

We are patient with ourselves in this process. We do not rush ourselves, yet we go ahead and make the amends as soon as we are able, one at a time. We may decide to write our amends on paper first to boost our confidence, and read from that. Most important is that we say our amends sincerely, and then take things as they come. We know we are taking an important step forward in our recovery. We might find helpful the program slogan *Live and let live.*

We keep the focus on our recovery

We remember that we are making amends to help us get well. We are not trying to change anyone else. We are not seeking amends from them in return. We do our best to approach our amends with an attitude of acceptance and forgiveness—both toward others and ourselves. We realize we are doing the best we can, and so are they. Our dual illnesses have likely thrown us both off balance. We let go of our judgments and resentments and keep the focus on our own recovery.

We also remember to make amends to ourselves. We forgive ourselves for having our illnesses. We forgive ourselves for the consequences and problems our dual illnesses have caused us. We recommit ourselves to recovery as a way of mending our relationship with ourselves and with our Higher Power. Changing to healthier living is often our best form of amends.

The tools to help us
A spirit of openness

Rather than approaching Step Nine with great fear, we adopt an attitude of welcoming the opportunity. Step Nine offers us a valuable chance to rebuild our lives. We keep in the front of our minds our vision of recovery, and we move toward it eagerly. We know this Step is a challenge, and alone we might falter. But we have the support of the Steps, our Higher Power, our sponsor, others in recovery, and our own internal resources to do what is before us. If we stumble, we will not fall. By calling on the support we need, we are able to stand up tall and go on, stronger for the experience.

The Serenity Prayer

Once again, the Serenity Prayer can help us make the most of a Step. We especially pay attention to the third line that asks for "the courage to change the things I can."

Barriers to overcome
Fear of rejection and pain

We may be reluctant to do Step Nine because we are afraid of how others will react. But we are often surprised by the way many people respond to us. Some will be quite understanding. They will appreciate our honesty and sincerity. They will respect what we are doing in recovery. Others will have already forgotten the incidents that bother us so much. Still others may show no interest in meeting with us or may even be apathetic about what we tell them. We may be met with anger, rejection, or a kind of skepticism that suggests, "I've heard all this before," "You just want something from me," "You just want my trust back," or "You are using me to get out of some kind of trouble." Under these circumstances, we do the best we can to make the amends and then let go of the outcome. We do not let the reactions of others disturb us. We turn to our Higher Power and others in recovery for support throughout the process of making our amends. We know that what we are doing is for our own recovery.

Unavailability of some people

If we cannot meet in person, we can write letters to the people affected. If they are no longer living or cannot be contacted, we can put in writing our sincere amends, even though we cannot mail them. We may find it helpful to share what we have written with our sponsor. But we make every effort to make personal contact with people from our past, at least by phone. If we are not able to locate some of the people, we keep them on our list. At some point during our recovery, we may meet them again and have the opportunity at that time.

Instability

Those of us with dual disorders have a special need to pay attention to our emotional well-being as we approach this process of making amends. When we do Step Nine, we want to be sure we are ready. We want to be sincere in our motives. We want our amends to be a part of the mending process with ourselves and others. Therefore, we consider our emotional state carefully. How long have I been working a dual recovery program with stability and quality? Are my symptoms well managed at this time? Have I experienced significant changes in my life recently? Am I in the process of making a change in my medication? Is this the right time to make amends?

We do not use these issues as an excuse to avoid Step Nine. Rather, we take this opportunity to use soundness of judgment in working our program. Each of us has to evaluate our own situation, with the help of our sponsor, our Higher Power, and our medical advisors. We don't want to risk bringing on more stress than we can manage. Some of us may need to wait until we have reached a greater level of stability in our psychiatric illness. We may need months or even a couple of years of quality dual recovery before we are well enough to make amends. If we have been traumatized by severe abuse, for example, we may need the help of a therapist before we feel safe enough to approach some people.

Legal problems

During episodes of illness or during intoxication, a few of us have broken the law. For some of us, encounters with the legal system may have been the turning point that lead us to recovery. It's important to use sound judgment when our amends involve legal matters. We may need to consult with legal counsel, case managers, or other appropriate professionals. We could face serious consequences. In some cases, prison sentences or restitution may be required. But the more important amends are in our heart and minds.

Benefits

Connection with others

For many of us, Step Nine is our first attempt to reach out and relate to others in a long time. Because of our dual disorders, we have felt alone and disconnected. With Step Nine, we are mending our sense of loss and separation. We take our first, perhaps stumbling, steps toward connecting with others. We are learning to live as part of our community and part of the world again. We are willing to risk the lumps and bumps of relationships. We are willing to forgive, live, and let live. We are also open to the joy that comes from mutual, honest, and caring relationships. Becoming part of a bigger whole, we feel more complete.

Strength and freedom

No longer bound by feelings of shame and guilt, we are flexing new muscles and feeling a new sense of strength. As we practice the new relationship skills of honesty, responsibility, and compassion, we find people give us room to do so. Many of them support us lovingly. With Step Nine, we find the freedom to be ourselves, and discover we can be accepted for who we are. We also become more accepting of others. This acceptance dissolves our judgment and resentment that has shut us off from others.

This internal strength is important. Recovery is an "inside job." It does not take away either of our illnesses. We will still experience some symptoms of our psychiatric or emotional illness. We will still have the urge, whether frequently or rarely, to use alcohol or other drugs. But with the internal strength from our recovery, we will not be overpowered by our symptoms. We can manage our illnesses and our lives sanely. We can stop fighting our illnesses, ourselves, and others who care about us.

Stepping forward

We have come a long way since we started our recovery. We have laid a solid foundation in the program. We know our strengths and the risks we face. We have made a commitment to change our ways. We have moved into action to clean up the past and reunite with the world. Our progress has been good, and we can see much yet that we want to do in order to realize our vision of recovery. The next three Steps help us make a plan for daily maintenance of our recovery and growth. In Step Ten, we begin with a plan for a daily inventory.

STEP TEN

Continued to take personal inventory and when wrong promptly admitted it, while continuing to recognize our progress in dual recovery.

In Step Ten, we learn how to maintain the gains we have experienced thus far in dual recovery and how to continue with our growth. If we have been sincere in working our program, we have begun to leave behind the liabilities and replace them with our assets. Step Ten helps us monitor our progress and keep moving in a positive direction.

Though we have made great progress already, we continue to be at risk because our dual illnesses are chronic. Step Ten is the first of three Steps that help us maintain ongoing sobriety and emotional stability. This maintenance includes an ongoing personal inventory and prompt admission every time our stinking thinking resurfaces. But our main focus is on noticing our progress. Otherwise, we tend to dwell on our negative feelings and experiences.

Why Step Ten is needed
We can slip into complacency

When we have completed our first nine Steps, we may be quite satisfied with ourselves and our progress. If we are staying sober and drug-free, if we are self-accepting and finding a spiritual serenity, and if our psychiatric symptoms are well managed, we may feel that we are finished with the main work of our recovery. We expect smooth sailing from here on. Yet this is far from the truth. Dual recovery is a daily program of change. Our liabilities include long-ingrained habits. We can easily return to old patterns of coping. A vigilant effort is needed to replace these liabilities. In addition, our assets take time to build and feel comfortable to us. A program of dual recovery is a lifelong process that eventually becomes a natural way of life for us. We are never truly finished.

After a few years, or even a few months, of recovery, we may start to feel lazy. We forget what we need to do. We get bored, busy, discouraged, sidetracked, or grandiose. We backslide into denial, our old way of coping. We think we don't need the program as much as we did when we were in the crisis that brought us to recovery. We start to think we can manage our illnesses by ourselves if they are under control now. This is a dangerous state of mind. The urge to use may recur and catch us off guard at a point when we are less able to cope with it. Our psychiatric symptoms may recur or intensify, and we will not be prepared to deal with them. We are like athletes who do not keep up with a regular exercise program, lose strength and flexibility, and become easily subject to injury when they are not up to the demand.

New challenges come up

As we grow in our dual recovery, many changes take place in our lives, and these changes bring us new challenges. Changing relationships and activities, even for the better, involves a process of adjustment. If we decide to choose different friends and to stay away from the places where we used to drink or use other drugs, we experience losses and feel tension as we adjust to these changes. If we decide to follow a new treatment regimen or if a medication change is required, we get frustrated and discouraged if we don't get the results we hoped for. We may experience uncomfortable side effects, or the medication may not work as expected.

These new challenges require that we continue on a regular basis to let go of coping patterns that we used to protect ourselves for so long. We also must continue to take hold of our assets and develop new ones. Step Ten helps us maintain a positive outlook and continue building our recovery.

Old memories come up

As we become more stabilized in our psychiatric illness and have an extended period of sobriety, we often start to think more clearly. Memories may surface about events that we were unable to recall when we did our Fourth Step. The Tenth Step helps us use those memories to strengthen our recovery. If possible, we promptly resolve any unfinished business related to these memories. A more comprehensive Step Four inventory may be required to resolve some memories. If so, we welcome the opportunity to explore these situations in depth and clear them up. If certain events have left psychological scars, we may seek the help of a therapist to fully resolve them, as they may directly relate to our psychiatric illness.

How Step Ten works
We do regular inventories

Step Ten provides a regular progress check on our recovery. We use the same process that we did in Steps Four through Nine any time we face a new challenge, small or large, in our recovery. Working Step Ten is much like watching a heart monitor: we look for any warning signs in our recovery. We take prompt action if we start to falter. We also watch for improvements that indicate we are on the right track, and we are alert to opportunities that can advance our recovery.

This progress check can be taken on a daily basis. Just as we did in Step Four, we notice if the symptoms of either of our dual disorders have been present, and we examine our reactions to any of these symptoms. We notice how we are feeling as we mend relationships and become active in our school, work, family life, community, or new relationships. We observe our beliefs, attitudes, and actions and note whether they are consistent with our values and the good, orderly direction that we have chosen for ourselves.

If we notice that we are putting less effort into building up our assets or if we find that we are slipping into stinking thinking, we acknowledge this right away. As in Step Five, we may talk over our progress with our sponsor and our Higher Power. We ask for any help we need to change the way we have been thinking and acting, calling on our assets as needed, just as we did in Steps Six and Seven. We find ourselves becoming as aware of the patterns in our recovery as we have long been aware of the patterns in our times of acute illness. Then, as in

Steps Eight and Nine, we make any necessary amends as soon as possible. We are patient with our progress and keep a positive focus.

Let's say we decide to discuss our emotional illness with friends or family and tell them specifically how they can be supportive when we are experiencing symptoms. Perhaps we have anxiety attacks, and we ask our loved ones to avoid giving us advice and to reassure us calmly that we will be all right when we are in the middle of an anxiety episode. But someone misunderstands what we say, thinks we are asking for sympathy, and accuses us of feeling sorry for ourselves. It would be very easy for us to become discouraged at this point. We might resort to self-defeating and self-destructive behavior, such as an outburst of rage, complete withdrawal, or even relapse.

Using Step Ten, we can instead notice our feelings of discouragement when they first start and discuss them with our sponsor and Higher Power. Just being honest about our feelings and having someone to listen might already reduce our stress and provide a feeling of relief. Next, we look to see if there is anything we can change to be more effective in the way we ask for what we want from those around us. We ask for guidance from our Higher Power to make these changes. Then if people were hurt (because, for example, we unfairly accused them of not doing enough for us), we make amends. Part of our amends is to reassure ourselves that we are not bad people or failures because this situation did not work out exactly as we had hoped. We do not assume that our mistakes are automatically a sign of an impending relapse. We commend ourselves for our courage in trying a new approach.

Three methods of inventory

There are three common methods for doing a Step Ten inventory. One is a *daily review checklist,* usually done at the beginning or end of the day. Choose a time of day when you can give the inventory full attention, and approach it with a positive outlook. For some people, morning is better, because by evening they may be tired and less able to examine themselves in the best light.

Inventories may be done formally in writing or informally as a mental review. Some people keep an organized checklist of their liabilities and assets by the bedside and briefly review them to determine their progress. Make plans to address any unresolved issues as soon as possible and draw on your assets to help you do so.

A *spot-check inventory* is another method for working Step Ten. During each day, reflect briefly on your liabilities and assets from time to time: How am I doing today? Take any needed action as soon as possible. If your stress level is rising, for example, slow down, breathe deeply, and try to take a break from the stressful situation. Do a brief inventory of your feelings and attitudes to see if a change is needed. If you feel an urge to use alcohol or other drugs, a spot-check inventory may remind you to call your sponsor. A spot-check inventory is a good way to catch yourself when you are at risk of relapse because you are *hungry, angry, lonely, or tired (HALT)*. If your day is going well, you can stop to take note of how well you are doing and acknowledge your gratitude to your source of help.

A *periodic inventory* is an occasional, more thorough, review of our liabilities and assets. You might take an hour or two, or even go away for a day-long retreat, to more fully evaluate your progress in dual recovery. Use this time to examine our overall patterns of thinking and acting, any unfinished business from your Fourth Step, and new directions you want to take.

The tools to help us

A journal

Writing our Step Ten inventory in a journal can help us in several ways. First, writing often clarifies our thinking. Also, just having the journal near the bedside is a regular reminder to do the inventory. Another benefit is having a written record that serves as an encouraging reminder of our progress over time. We can use our journal as a place to write our daily plans. This will help establish more order in our lives. Later, when we do our inventory, we can review these plans to see how we have done. Committing ourselves on paper holds us to the task. We are more likely to stay on track, to move forward—and less likely to go backward.

An attitude of openness

Step Ten reminds us that recovery from both illnesses is a matter of progress, not perfection. We see that our progress is sometimes rapid, sometimes gradual, and sometimes prompted by specific events. Step Ten helps us stay open to new discoveries about ourselves every day. It keeps us humble, reminding us of assets and alerting us to liabilities. We keep our expectations for dual recovery realistic.

Barriers to overcome
Grandiosity

As we are grow stronger in our recovery, we may become grandiose about our progress. Everything seems under control, and we no longer feel as if we are doing everything wrong. This development is understandable. Before we began dual recovery, everything did seem to be wrong. Because we were impaired by our dual illnesses, many times we could not cope or communicate effectively. Then, during treatment and recovery, we received a great deal of encouragement. Eventually we became stable and sober. We discovered that we were not bad people who were always in the wrong as we had thought.

After being "wrong" for so long, we now want to avoid this label entirely, along with the related guilt and shame. We fear that any sign of our wrongdoing means that we have failed and that we are going back to being "wrong" and miserable again. Denial has been a natural and automatic way of coping with distress. We are trying to protect our self-image and our feelings in the way we used to. If building our assets seems difficult, we fall back on the familiar liabilities.

Keeping an attitude of humility and openness is important in Step Ten. We recognize our progress, but that progress invariably includes making some mistakes. We acknowledge those errors and take responsibility for them, confident that all is not lost and that we are growing stronger as we meet each challenge with courage and honesty.

Step Ten

Discouragement

Not everything gets better when we are in recovery. Our marriage may be too far gone to save. We may have trouble returning to work. We may have difficulty finding and adjusting to the right medications quickly. Yet none of these difficulties are a sign of failed recovery. Recovery means that we strive to respond positively to whatever is going on around us. When external circumstances are not going well for us, we use Step Ten to build confidence by reminding ourselves of our assets and repeatedly drawing on them to replace our liabilities. We do the best we can, and we know that is good enough.

We have been caught up for so long in the symptoms of our dual disorders and their consequences and problems that much of our energy has been directed toward coping with negative experiences at every turn. Disturbances in health, family life, work, friendships—it seems that virtually everything has been a source of pain and chaos. Seeing negatives has become a way of life. Step Ten asks us for a change in perspective, reminding us to continue "to recognize our progress in dual recovery."

Benefits

Improved quality of life

It is so easy to feel miserable if our illnesses and our lives get out of control. Step Ten helps us stop feeling bad. Through our ongoing personal inventory, we are better able to manage our dual disorders because we can spot any problems as they come up and quickly draw upon our assets to address them. We also keep building on our assets and use them to continuously improve the quality of our lives.

Long-term recovery

Our dual disorders are long-term illnesses that we learn to manage on a day-to-day basis. We need long-term recovery. Step Ten is one of three Steps that help us sustain that recovery. It is a source of hope. Without Step Ten, we could so easily be devastated by the reappearance of liabilities. Assets could be quickly forgotten or overshadowed. But we have Step Ten to keep us going in the direction of recovery. It is a concrete, sensible step. Those of us who make a habit of practicing Step Ten never stay down for long. The promise of recovery is as close as our inventory.

Stepping forward

In Step Ten, we routinely check how well our recovery is going and make any needed adjustments. As we move forward to Step Eleven, we have the opportunity to get well acquainted with our Higher Power to help us make these adjustments and guide us in the direction of greater recovery.

STEP ELEVEN

Sought through prayer and meditation to improve our conscious contact with our Higher Power, praying only for knowledge of our Higher Power's will for us and the power to carry that out.

In Step Eleven, we continue to work with our source of help to build our recovery in a self-loving way. We chose our Higher Power in Step Two and decided to use the care and guidance of this source of help in Step Three. In Step Seven, we asked for support to stop relying on our liabilities. But how can we continue to work with our source of help on an ongoing basis? How do we keep in touch for care, support, and, guidance? How do we find the power to follow through on the guidance we are given? Step Eleven suggests that we seek this knowledge and power through a time of reflection described in traditional language as prayer and meditation. In other words, we find a direct way to stay in contact with and listen to our source of help.

Why Step Eleven is needed
We forget where our help comes from

After we have been in dual recovery for a time, it's very tempting to return to the belief that we can manage our disorders and our lives by ourselves. In the beginning, we worked with our source of help extensively to lead us to a saner, more useful life. Now we may feel stronger and more confident and assume we can make it on our own. Our memories of the crises and pain that brought us into the program grow distant and fuzzy. We forget the tremendous despair we once felt and the enormous effort it took to get this far. We take for granted our present sense of well-being, forgetting that the foundation we have laid must be maintained.

How wonderful that we feel much better! Yet what has brought us this far is the guidance of our Higher Power. That guidance continues to be necessary if we are to maintain our recovery and continue growing.

We are uncertain what to do

We are faced with many decisions—big and small—every day in the process of our recovery. How should we best manage our psychiatric symptoms and our urge to drink or use drugs? How should we respond when we encounter the prejudice others have about mental illness and chemical dependency? What can we do to motivate ourselves when we feel down? Who should we spend time with today? What would the most responsible living arrangement be? Who should we trust? All of these decisions affect our recovery, either positively or negatively. They can overwhelm us when we feel alone and have no clear sense of direction. We might feel frozen in panic and withdraw. We might lash out at someone when we get confused or when we don't see promising solutions to our problems. Even when we make a decision, we may second-guess ourselves, wondering if we did the right thing. These reactions are often based on stinking thinking or other liabilities. Ongoing distress, confusion, and anxiety can put us at risk for relapse.

Step Eleven helps us learn how to draw upon our source of help to guide us through life's daily decisions. Many of us call on our Higher Power for guidance often during the day.

How Step Eleven works

We seek knowledge of our Higher Power's will

In the course of our illnesses, we have tried repeatedly to change the people and conditions around us, to make them conform to what we wanted. We wanted to use alcohol or other drugs on our own terms, and we wanted everyone to leave us alone so we could use them without interference. We tried to control our emotional illness. We tried to get the people who cared for us to see things our way. We became angry or withdrawn when things didn't go our way.

In dual recovery, we match our desires with those of our Higher Power. Rather than trying to make the world or the program conform to us, our mission becomes shaping ourselves to our program of recovery. Our Higher Power shows us the way. In Step Eleven, we make a conscious effort to become aware of our Higher Power and seek its direction. We look beyond ourselves to the big picture. We try to answer these questions: What will keep me on the path of recovery? What will help me grow? What values are important to live by? How do I move ahead in the direction I have already chosen? What do I have to contribute? What is my role in life? How can I become more sensitive to the needs of others and the world we live in? How can I learn better skills to communicate with others and cope more effectively?

In addition to looking at the big picture, we also seek guidance in even the smallest day-to-day matters. How should I deal with my son's anger? What can I do to cope when my car breaks down? Should I apply for the assistant manager position that just opened up at work? Should I go out for coffee with my friends or stay home and rest?

We seek the power to carry out the direction we receive

When we understand what our source of help is directing us to do, we may quickly slip into self-doubt. How can we possibly do what we need to do? Again, we work with our source of help to discover the power to do what has to be done. We find that our greatest source of power lies within. We remember that we have come this far because our will to survive has triumphed over our dual disorders. We have already made the most fundamental choice—to get better, to have a good life—and we have acted on that choice with courage. Now we become willing to grow in courage, hope, motivation, and involvement by working with our source of help.

We make conscious contact with our Higher Power

In the spiritual tradition, prayer and meditation are the most common ways of making contact with the Higher Power known by names such as God, Allah, or Great Spirit. Prayer is talking to our Higher Power. Meditation is a time of quiet reflection and listening, gaining understanding and direction from what our Higher Power says.

There are many forms of prayer and meditation. Whatever form we use, we try to take some time by ourselves each day, preferably in a quiet setting, specifically for this time of conversation and reflection. Some of us use written prayers from a religious tradition. Or we may talk informally with our Higher Power, expressing thoughts, desires, and feelings—including any anger we might feel toward our Higher Power—and asking for direction. When we meditate, we may focus on our breathing or on some object or word that calms us. We use whatever means helps us to be receptive to the inner guiding voice of our Higher Power, a voice that inspires courage, serenity, acceptance, and a positive sense of direction.

Those of us who chose a source of help not connected with a spiritual tradition also take time for quiet reflection. We go for a walk or lie on the bed or sit in a favorite chair and consider these questions. We read from program literature or from other inspirational materials. We recall the words and ideas we have heard from our source of help, whether that is our group, our medical team, the Steps themselves, or another source. What is important is to make a conscious effort to grow in awareness of our Higher Power and stay in ongoing contact.

In our time of reflection, we often find that distracting thoughts pass through our minds. This is normal. We do not criticize ourselves for anything we hear, see, or feel. We simply notice what happens and calmly go back to our point of focus. As we open ourselves to receiving guidance, we distinguish the voice of our Higher Power from any other voices or thoughts that come along by looking for positive, caring messages. If because of our psychiatric illness, we hear disturbing voices or see upsetting visions during our time of reflection, we talk over these experiences with our doctor.

We try to set aside this time of quiet reflection daily. Much like an athlete who physically and mentally prepares for a game, we stay strong and focused by using our prayer and meditation exercises. We can also do Step Eleven in conjunction with Step Ten, using part of our quiet time to take an inventory of our liabilities and assets and note our progress.

Contact with our Higher Power is not limited to any specific activity or time we set aside, however. We can go within ourselves anytime to connect with a sense of deep serenity, knowing we are continually cared for and guided. We may experience an awareness of our Higher Power when we hear a toddler's full-hearted laughter or when we stroke a kitten or smell a carnation. We may use an artistic or physical form of prayer and meditation, such as playing a musical instrument or practicing the martial arts. There are many ways for us to make the connection with our source of help if we are willing to become aware. We become aware and ask, become aware and listen, become aware and act.

The tools to help us
Tapes, books, music, journal

We find many tools to help us with our time of reflection. Inspirational music or books may uplift us. We may listen to tapes that offer encouraging messages or guided meditations. Writing in a journal or reviewing previous uplifting entries may be of help. We might go to a favorite outdoor spot where nature can inspire us. We might use positive imagery—imagining ourselves as we would like to be, in harmony with our Higher Power, and then expressing our belief that we already becoming that way.

Affirmations

Some of us use *affirmations,* positive statements about ourselves, to reinforce caring messages from our Higher Power. We say these at special times during the day, and we post them as reminders at homes, in the car, and in the workplace. Examples of affirmations include the following:

- I am relaxed, calm, and at peace.
- I am a good person, and I am doing the best I can.
- I can manage my dual disorders and my life with the help of my Higher Power.
- When I experience my symptoms, I am still okay on the inside.

- I have the courage and strength to meet today's challenges.
- With joy, I turn my will and my life over to the care of my Higher Power.

An attitude of gratitude

We have much to be grateful for in our dual recovery. We are feeling and functioning far better than we could have imagined when we started in recovery. Our relationships have improved. We have developed new abilities or built up existing ones. We have higher self-esteem. We have been helped a great deal by our Higher Power, by many caring people, and by our own will to live. An attitude of gratitude is a good way to approach Step Eleven. It will help us open up to even more of the gifts that recovery has to offer.

Barriers to overcome

Lack of know-how or experience

Some of us feel awkward at the thought of spending time in quiet reflection making contact with our Higher Power. We have not done it before, or perhaps we are uncomfortable with anything that seems religious. But just as we've become adept at other new skills, such as doing an inventory or making amends, we can learn to pray and meditate with practice and with help from others. We are encouraged when we look around and see the benefits others in recovery have experienced from Step Eleven. We want those benefits and are willing to try different reflection practices until we find what is comfortable and effective for us. We may find that these practices are not as foreign to us as we had anticipated. If we enjoy nature or are inspired by an uplifting speaker, we already have a sense of what it means to connect with our Higher Power. We have connected with the message—a positive belief we share with others. We start with that and add more as we come to desire more recovery. *Easy does it* is a good slogan to keep in mind as we learn these new practices.

Some of us experience psychiatric symptoms that make it difficult for us to maintain an extended period of quiet reflection. Our attention span is short, and we become agitated. We don't let this keep us from the benefits of Step Eleven. We seek guidance from our Higher Power, our sponsor, and others in recovery about how to work the Step effectively. We may find we can become aware of our Higher Power while remaining physically active. Perhaps we choose more frequent but briefer opportunities to go within and seek guidance. We do whatever works best for our recovery.

If we are bothered by the traditional connection of prayer and meditation with religion, we remember that we are the ones who chose our Higher Power. What we name this practice of quiet reflection and connection with our Higher Power is unimportant. What matters is that we find some way to increase our awareness and working relationship with our source of help, a way that genuinely makes sense to us and helps us.

Belief that Step Eleven is unnecessary

Some of us, at first, resist the idea of praying and meditating. We think it is stupid or unnecessary. We conclude that working Step Three was enough. Since we are sober and the symptoms of our emotional or psychiatric illness are under control, we wonder why we should bother with the idea of a Higher Power any further. But we forget that our recovery goals also include maintaining our recovery and preventing relapse. Working with our source of help doesn't stop with Step Three. As a matter of fact, in order to work a good Step Three, we need to establish and maintain connection with our Higher Power so that we are clear about what guidance to follow. Recovery is a daily program. We seek ongoing guidance using Step Eleven, and we follow that guidance using Step Three.

Benefits

A sense of balance

Step Eleven helps us keep our lives in balance. By continually staying in touch with our source of help and following the direction we are given, we keep a sane and sound perspective on our dual disorders. We make wise choices. Over time, we begin to notice that we no longer experience the extreme ups and downs that were once so familiar to us. We are calmer. We trust ourselves more. We find we are in tune with our inner self, our program of dual recovery, the people in our lives, and the many resources we have available.

Ability to stay focused on recovery

When everything seems to be going well, how easy it is to forget about the gains we have made with the help of our Higher Power and our program. We may also forget our progress when we are in the middle of a crisis. We become too busy or too preoccupied to call on the resources of the program at these times. Step Eleven, along with the other maintenance Steps, keeps us focused on our dual recovery day in and day out. We develop a natural routine, just as anyone who is ill follows a routine of medication or other treatments. We make a habit of working with our Higher Power's guidance, and that guidance sustains us through good times and bad. We remain clear, confident, and positive in our dual recovery. We know we will be able to cope with the help of our Higher Power, no matter what happens.

Stepping forward

If we honestly practice the skills and suggestions offered in Step Eleven, nothing can hold us back in our recovery. We have the many resources of the program to call on. We are connected to our Higher Power, a constant source of help we can trust. Our outlook on life is stronger and brighter. We find such excitement in our progress that we want it to fill every corner of our lives. We also want to share it with others. Step Twelve gives us that opportunity.

STEP TWELVE

Having had a spiritual awakening as the result of these Steps, we tried to carry this message to others who experience dual disorders and to practice these principles in all our affairs.

Step Twelve suggests that as we experience constructive changes through the program of dual recovery, we try to help others and to apply what we have learned in all areas of our lives. We have stopped the deadly progression of our dual disorders and reversed the downward spiral of consequences, problems, and denial. We have set in motion a program that helps us cope positively with our urge to use and our tendency to give up on ourselves when life becomes unmanageable. Our awareness and our attitudes have changed for the better. The quality of our lives has improved significantly. In Step Twelve, we broaden and deepen the changes we have experienced by continually applying the principles of dual recovery in every area of our lives. Recovery becomes a way of life.

We have learned from experience that the only way to keep our recovery strong is to share it with others. We help them and we help ourselves at the same time.

Why Step Twelve is needed
A vigorous program keeps us growing

What we have gained in dual recovery is so rich, we want to keep it growing. We keep finding new ways to practice the principles of the program in small matters and large. The more we read about these principles and deepen our understanding of them, the more we talk about these ideas with others in dual recovery, reflect on them, and act on them, the more our lives improve. Step Twelve reminds us of the growth we have experienced and invites us to enjoy even more benefits.

We might think we can manage alone once we have a good understanding of dual recovery and enough successful experience to bring our symptoms under control. But experience has shown that quality, long-term recovery improves through working the program along with others. Alone, we may grow complacent and bored and slip into denial. We also need a sounding board to help us celebrate our successes and cope with our challenges in recovery. Joining with others in recovery helps us stay honest, positive, and on course. At the same time, the program is kept fresh and alive from the collective knowledge and experience of everyone involved.

We could go backward

Having come so far in recovery, we are frightened at the thought of slipping into relapse. That fear is healthy because it helps us stay motivated. We must rely on Step Twelve, along with the other maintenance Steps, to keep us on a sure course of dual recovery.

Others with dual disorders are hurting

Many others are suffering the same despair and chaos from their dual disorders that we once experienced. Step Twelve provides us the opportunity to share with them our experience, strength, and hope. We help others, just as we have been helped.

How Step Twelve works
We recognize and expand our spiritual awakening

As a result of working the program, we have a brighter and broader outlook on life. We have a solid inner strength and serenity that sustain us regardless of any chaos going on around us. We have a more complete and honest picture of our liabilities and assets. We have gone from feeling useless and hopeless to making concrete improvements in our living situation, relationships, and work. We have gone from feeling we should get into recovery to wanting recovery. Our self-respect has grown. We no longer feel victims of our dual disorders. We may not be fully aware of it, but we have realized a spiritual awakening.

Some of the changes have been dramatic. Perhaps we enrolled in school, began to take our family responsibilities seriously, or started a new treatment plan. Other changes were more subtle. Maybe we are less anxious around other people or more willing to listen to the opinions of others. Some changes we only notice when others mention that we are acting different. We feel good about these changes. We keep strengthening and expanding our efforts in dual recovery, confident of more beneficial changes down the road.

We carry the message

We continue our growth by sharing as well as by listening. Whether we are new to the program or have years of experience, we all have something important and valuable to share. Each person's growth offers hope and strength to others in recovery. We are often unaware how each and every small act of service or the honest sharing of our experience has touched someone else. If even one person is helped by our efforts, we have done a great service.

We have many opportunities for sharing the message. We can

- visit someone with a dual disorder in a treatment center, halfway house, or detox center and tell our story of recovery
- participate in a Twelve Step group for people with dual disorders
- tell our story at open meetings
- share our growth with others at closed meetings
- provide service to our group by answering phones or by helping with meetings or other events
- sponsor others in the program
- write our stories for others to read

We are careful not to put ourselves at risk as we work with others who may still be using alcohol or other drugs or who are experiencing an episode of their emotional or psychiatric illness. We take care of our physical and emotional well-being. We use common sense. We do what we can for others, but if others are not receptive to our message or become a threat to themselves or others, we may call on professionals or other caregivers to intervene. We allow others to choose recovery when they are ready.

In carrying the message of dual recovery to others, we are careful not to preach or tell them what they should believe. We do not diagnose their illness or act as a consultant on their treatment. We are not gurus or professionals in dual recovery, but men and women who share the common experience of being affected by dual disorders. We show compassion and concern for others and share with them our experience, strength, and hope. We speak from the heart, with humility and gratitude. The best way we have found to carry the message is to live it rather than just talk about it.

We practice the principles

Over time, the principles of dual recovery become so attractive to us that almost automatically they spill over into other areas of our lives. We conduct ourselves more honestly in our relationships. We become more responsible with our money. We show greater integrity at school or work. We find ourselves becoming more comfortable with ourselves, our illnesses, and our world.

The tools to help us

Program resources

We have many tools to help us as we continue on in recovery. Program literature, meetings, and sponsors are essential. We keep a journal to record our progress and to help us sort out difficult situations. We use the telephone to call our sponsor and others in the program. We keep in mind the Serenity Prayer, and we practice the slogans of recovery such as *One day at a time, Live and let live,* and *Keep it simple.* We know we are never alone or without support.

Those who care about us

As we grow in the program, our relationships become healthier and more supportive. We are able to give and receive love. We grow in our ability to trust those close to us. As we become more honest, we learn to welcome honesty from others around us. Others who know us can be very helpful in giving us feedback about our recovery, if we are open to hearing what they say. We also are better able to ask for the kind of support we need in our recovery. We do not limit our contacts to people who are in recovery in an attempt to hide from the rest of the world. Any healthy relationship can be beneficial.

Barriers to overcome
Complacency

After a time in the program, we are apt to experience periods of feeling bored, tired, busy, or lazy concerning our program. We tend to forget how disabling and even life-threatening our dual disorders can be. The three maintenance Steps help us to counteract complacency. In Step Twelve, we are reminded that we need a daily program to maintain life-long recovery and prevent relapse. We find that we can only keep our recovery if we give it away.

Problems with personalities

We might find ourselves getting impatient with some of the other people in dual recovery. Their personalities may rub us the wrong way. We start to judge their progress. We feel let down when our sponsor is not always a shining example of recovery. Yet we try to remember to keep the focus on our own recovery. We work the principles for ourselves, and we accept that others are responsible for their own recovery. We try to remember that we each have our own needs and strengths and that we each use our assets in different ways. Some make progress quickly, others more slowly. We take from others what will help us, and we leave the rest. We accept others where they are, just as we want to be accepted.

Benefits
Safety and serenity

Dual recovery becomes a safe way of life for us. We are supported and encouraged and empowered. We know we can be ourselves and be accepted just as we are. We are pursuing new, self-loving directions for ourselves. We are aware of our assets and we know how to put them into action. We are aware of our liabilities, and we are learning how to lessen them. We are in contact with a Higher Power that we have chosen ourselves, and we can work with this source of help at all times. We have strengthened our relationships, and we feel more connected to people. When our symptoms recur, we take measures to help ourselves, including reaching out for others more quickly than we used to. The quality of our lives has improved. We experience more harmony and balance than we have known in a long time, perhaps ever. We feel confident that even if others bombard us with stigma and prejudice because of our dual disorders, we are strong. We know we are good people with two no-fault illnesses. We have others who will support us when we feel unsteady. Living with such a feeling of safety gives us a deep serenity. Despite turmoil around us, we are at peace.

Feeling part of something larger
Working our program of dual recovery is more than a personal process. We are part of something larger. We contribute to the recovery of others. Our involvement in dual recovery contributes to the deepening and strengthening of the whole program.

Stepping forward
With these Twelve Steps as our guide, we move forward in life with direction and balance. We trust ourselves, our Higher Power, and our program to help us cope in a healthy way with our dual disorders.

THE TWELVE STEPS OF
ALCOHOLICS ANONYMOUS*

1. We admitted we were powerless over alcohol—that our lives had become unmanageable.
2. Came to believe that a Power greater than ourselves could restore us to sanity.
3. Made a decision to turn our will and our lives to the care of God *as we understood Him.*
4. Made a searching and fearless inventory of ourselves.
5. Admitted to God, to ourselves, and to another human being the exact nature of our wrongs.
6. Were entirely ready to have God remove all these defects of character.
7. Humbly asked Him to remove our shortcomings.
8. Made a list of all persons we had harmed, and became willing to make amends to them all.
9. Made direct amends to such people wherever possible, except when to do so would injure them or others.
10. Continued to take personal inventory and when we were wrong promptly admitted it.
11. Sought through prayer and meditation to improve our conscious contact with God *as we understood Him,* praying only for knowledge of His will for us and the power to carry that out.
12. Having had a spiritual awakening as the result of these steps, we tried to carry this message to alcoholics and to practice these principles in all our affairs.

---

*The Twelve Steps of AA are taken from *Alcoholics Anonymous,* 3d ed., published by AA World Services, Inc., New York, N.Y., 59-60. Reprinted with permission of AA World Services, Inc. (See editor's note on copyright page.)

THE TWELVE STEPS OF
DUAL RECOVERY ANONYMOUS*

1. We admitted we were powerless over our dual illness of chemical dependency and emotional or psychiatric illness—that our lives had become unmanageable.

2. Came to believe that a Higher Power of our understanding could restore us to sanity.

3. Made a decision to turn our will and our lives over to the care of our Higher Power, to help us to rebuild our lives in a positive and caring way.

4. Made a searching and fearless personal inventory of ourselves.

5. Admitted to our Higher Power, to ourselves, and to another human being, the exact nature of our liabilities and our assets.

6. Were entirely ready to have our Higher Power remove all our liabilities.

7. Humbly asked our Higher Power to remove these liabilities and to help us to strengthen our assets for recovery.

8. Made a list of all persons we had harmed and became willing to make amends to them all.

9. Made direct amends to such people wherever possible, except when to do so would injure them or others.

10. Continued to take personal inventory and when wrong promptly admitted it, while continuing to recognize our progress in dual recovery.

11. Sought through prayer and meditation to improve our conscious contact with our Higher Power, praying only for knowledge of our Higher Power's will for us and the power to carry that out.

12. Having had a spiritual awakening as a result of these Steps, we tried to carry this message to others who experience dual disorders and to practice these principles in all our affairs.

---

*Adapted from the Twelve Steps of Alcoholics Anonymous. The Twelve Steps of Dual Recovery Anonymous are used with the permission of the Dual Recovery Anonymous Central Service Office, P.O. Box 8107, Prairie Village, Kansas 66208.

About the Authors

R. W. Tim Hamilton is the founder and director of Dual Recovery Network Association, an organization that offers education, advocacy, and self-help support to people with dual disorders and their family members. He has worked in the field of chemical dependency counseling and education since 1974, and is a contributing author to Hazelden's *The Dual Disorders Recovery Book*.

Pat Samples is a freelance writer who has published many magazine articles, a book on chronic mental illness, and several Hazelden works, including *Self-Care for Caregivers: A Twelve Step Approach*. She lives in Minneapolis and is actively involved in Twelve Step programs.

More support for dual disorder recovery...

The Dual Disorders Recovery Book

A Twelve Step Program for Those of Us with Addiction and An Emotional or Psychiatric Illness

This is a basic, realistic, inspirational source of information, shared experience, and relapse prevention help to those living with both chemical addiction and a psychiatric disorder. In easy-to-understand language, this book explains the relationship between emotional or psychiatric disorders and chemical dependency. Personal stories share the struggle of coping with dual disorders and reinforce long-term recovery maintenance. 250 pp.

Order No. 1500

Preventing Relapse *(Co-Occuring workbook)*
by Dennis C. Daley, M.S.W.

Designed for the person recovering from dual disorders, this workbook encourages an ongoing examination of personal behavior and recovery. The exercises help you create a relapse prevention plan for handling risky situations relating to both your addiction and psychiatric or emotional condition—a plan that you can refer to whenever needed. 32 pp.

Order No. 2162

Embracing the Fear

Learning to Manage Anxiety and Panic Attacks
by Judith Bemis and Amr Barrada

Anxiety disorders are among the most common types of mental health problems among adults in the United States today. Whether you're living with a steady level of mild anxiety, phobias, panic attacks, or disabling agoraphobia, this book provides methods to manage anxiety and change the way you think and act. 160 pp.

Order No. 1510

For price and order information, or a free catalog, please call our Telephone Representatives.

HAZELDEN

1-800-328-9000	**1-651-213-4000**	**1-651-213-4590**
(Toll Free U.S., Canada, and the Virgin Islands)	(Outside the U.S. and Canada)	(24-Hour FAX) http://www.hazelden.org

Pleasant Valley Road • P.O. Box 176 • Center City, MN 55012-0176